JOURNEYS

READING

2

RONI LEBAUER

STEVEN BROWN SERIES EDITOR

Prentice Hall Asia ELT

Publishing Director: Stephen Troth
Acquisitions Editor: Nancy Baxer
Design/Illustrations: Betty Bravo, Marketing Horizons
Production Manager: Oliver Lam

First published 1997 by
Prentice Hall Asia ELT
317 Alexandra Road
#04-01 IKEA Building
Singapore 159965

Printed in Singapore

Library of Congress Cataloging-in-Publication Data

Information is available from the publisher on request.

ISBN 0-13-180332-8 (Journeys Reading 2)

5 4 3 2 1
99 98 97

Contents

Reprint Permissions and References

Unit 1   "I'll Never Forget...What's-His-Name" from "Memory" by Kalia Doner, *American Health*, March 1994, pp. 58–60.

Unit 2   "Martina Navratilova: On and Off the Tennis Court" from "Game, Set, Match" by *Time*, vol. 142, no. 15, October 11, 1992, p. 93; and from "The Lioness in Winter" in *Time*, vol. 140, no. 22, November 30, 1992, p. 62.

Unit 3   "Take Two Bowls and Call Me in the Morning" from "Take Two Bowls and Call Me in the Morning" by Charles Perry in *LA Times*, April 2, 1993, p. H32.

Unit 4   "Why We Keep Going to McDonald's" from "Why We Keep Going to McDonald's" by Penny Moser, *Fortune*, © 1988 Time Inc. All rights reserved.

Unit 7   "Building Down Not Up" from "Notes from the Underground" by Fred Hapgood in *The Atlantic Monthly*, August 1994, pp. 34–38 and "Super-rise Party" in *Utne Reader*, Jan/Feb 1994, pp. 24–25.

Unit 9   "Don't Worry, Be Happy" lyrics by Bobby McFerrin, permission granted by Prob Noblem Music; permission granted for picture of Bobby McFerrin by Carol Friedman; "The Winter Blues" from "Shedding Dietary Light on Seasonal Affective Disorder" in *Tufts University Diet and Nutrition Letter*, vol. 12, no. 1, March 1994.

Unit 10   "Bums in the Attic," "A House of My Own" from *The House on Mango Street* © by Sandra Cisneros 1984. Published by Vintage Books, a division of Random House, Inc., NY in 1991 and in hardcover by Alfred A. Knopf in 1994; "Allowance" by James Masao Mitsui courtesy of Bieler Press, Marina del Rey, California.

Unit 11   Information from "The Baby Name Personality Survey" by Bruce Lansky and Barry Sinrod, NY: Meadowbrook Press, 1990; "Naming Names Around the World from Small World: A History of Baby Care from Stone Age to Spock Age" by Joan Bel Geddes, NY: Macmillan, 1964; Challenge questions adapted from "The Parent's Book of Facts: Child Development from Birth to Age Five" by Tom & Nancy Biracree, NY: Facts on File, Inc., 1989.

Unit 12   "Just a Kid? Look Again" from "Child Genius Searches for Cure to Parkinson's Disease" by Toska Zomorodian in *New University* (University of California, Irvine, newspaper), May 30, 1994, pp. 5 & 7, and from "Laguna Hills Prodigy has Prodigious Plans" by J Michael Kennedy in *LA Times*, May 23, 1994, pp. B1–B2.

Unit 13   "Help Her. Write Now," permission to reprint by Save the Children; "Hotel Housekeeper Makes Sparkling Discovery at Work" from "Hotel Housekeeper Makes Sparkling Discovery at Work." Reprinted by permission of The Orange County Register © 1994.

Unit 14   "Memories of Charlie" from "Charles the Great" by Claire Bloom in *Vogue*, vol. 182, no. 12, December 1992, pp. 114 & 120.

Unit 16   "My First Job" from "My First Job" in *Reader's Digest*, January 1993, pp. 161–168. Reprinted with permission from The Reader's Digest. © 1993 The Reader's Digest Assn., Inc.

Unit 17   "Your 'I' Says a Lot" from "Success Through Handwriting Analysis" by Malcolm W. Ater, Brookline MA: Brandon Publishing Co., 1985, pp. 26–27.

Unit 19   "Are You a Giraffe?" from The Giraffe Project, P. O. Box 759, Langley WA 98260.

Unit 20   "Early Song" from "Night Perimeter, New & Selected Poems 1958–1990" in *Greenview Review Press*, 1991; also "Fog" from "Chicago Poems" by Carl Sandburg, © 1916 by Holt, Rinehart, and Winston, Inc. and renewed 1944 by Carl Sandburg. Reprinted by permission of Harcourt Brace and Company.

The author and publishers are grateful for permissions to use copyright materials. It has not been possible to identify the sources of some of the materials used in this book and in such cases the publishers would welcome information from copyright owners.

Photo Credits

AP/Wide World Photos (p. 14 Martina Navratilova)

British Tourist Authority, Singapore (p. 25 I go to a fancy restaurant; p. 35 Stonehenge)

India Tourist Office, Singapore (p. 35 Taj Mahal)

Lam Wai Ling (p. 35 Eiffel Tower)

Nick Lutz (p. 128 Arturo Velez)

From the Series Editor

Journeys is a twelve-book, three-level, skills-based series for EFL/ESL learners. The books can be used from beginning level through intermediate level. They parallel the first three levels of basal series, and can be used as supplements to series or as stand-alone skills texts. A unique feature of *Journeys* is that the books can be used to construct a curriculum in those cases where student skills are at different levels. That is, in those classes where reading ability is at a higher level than speaking ability, the teacher is free to choose texts at appropriate levels. Each book can be used separately.

Journeys can be used with high-school-aged students and up.

Journeys takes three notions very seriously:

1. Beginning level students have brains and hearts. They live in an interesting world that they are interested in.

2. Learning needs to be recycled. Rather than work on the same skill or topic across all four books during the same week, topics and language are recycled across the books to keep what students have learned active. Teachers who want to can teach the books out of order because the syllabus of each book progresses slowly.

3. It is possible for beginning level students to work with sophisticated content, yet complete simple tasks. In general, students can understand a much higher level of language than they can produce. By grading tasks, that is, keeping them simple at a beginning level, the linguistic demands made of the students are kept relatively low, but the content of the exercises remains interesting to adult learners.

Steven Brown
Youngstown State University

Acknowledgements

Interacting with people from other cultures and learning from those interactions have always been, for me, important parts of my "journeys." Often these interactions are "on the road," but as an English Language teacher, I am also fortunate that I can have these contacts on a daily basis — in my classroom, as I teach and learn from my students. My first acknowledgement goes to my students, the many hundreds of students, who have met me at different crossroads and added so much to my understanding of the world and appreciation of our human diversity and similarity. They have truly inspired me.

My heartfelt thanks also go to the many people who have left their professional mark on this book — colleagues, artists, researchers. In particular, I'd like to express my gratitude to Suriani Osman, Lee Ming Ang, and Oliver Lam of the editorial and production staff at Prentice Hall Asia, to Betty Bravo and her art team, to Steven Brown (for his thoughtful, calm, and knowledgeable guidance as series editor), and to Nancy Baxer (for her unflagging dedication to and enthusiasm on this "journey").

Finally, my thanks go to my family and friends for all that they add to my "journeys." In particular, I am grateful for Michelle Rene-Ryan, for all that she gives: encouragement, food for thought, advice, laughter, support, understanding.

Roni Lebauer

How's your memory? Do you have a good memory for names? What about faces? Try this exercise and see. Look at the 9 pictures on page 137 for 1 minute. Try to remember the names and faces.

Now write the names under the correct pictures without looking at page 137. How many can you remember?

_____ _____ _____

_____ _____ _____

_____ _____ _____

Talk to a classmate and ask these questions:

On a scale of 1 to 4, how is your memory for people's faces?

1 VERY BAD   4 VERY GOOD

On a scale of 1 to 4, how is your memory for people's names?

1 VERY BAD   4 VERY GOOD

Do you have ways to help yourself remember names? If so, how?

READING 1.1

Dear Reader,

1   I'd like to introduce myself. My name is Roni Lebauer and I'm the author of your book. In addition to writing, I also teach at a college in Southern California.

2   I don't know what your class is like but I'd like to tell you a little about my classes. As you can see by the drawing, my classes are pretty big — about 45 students. It's hard to talk about a typical student because my students come from practically everywhere. This semester, I have students from Iran, Syria, France, Mexico, Bolivia, Guatemala, Vietnam, Hong Kong, Taiwan, Korea, Poland. Did I forget anyone? Perhaps.

3   At the beginning of the semester, I try to learn my students' names. It's not easy. (I usually have two other classes to learn as well.) I use a number of techniques to help myself remember. During the first week, I often ask my students to introduce themselves. After they speak, I ask other students questions about what they heard. They try to remember and I do, too. I also repeat names often out loud and to myself.

4   Would you like to know a little about some of my students? Let's see. There's Ana Maria. She's the young woman sitting in the back row with the striped shirt — the one with the shoulder-length brown hair. She's from Mexico. She studied to be a nurse in Mexico and now she hopes to continue her studies in the U.S. And that older gentleman with the glasses in the front row. He's Abu Taleb. He's 73 years old and loves school. He's retired but in Iran, he was a pharmacist. And Linh? She's the middle-aged Vietnamese woman sitting next to Abu Taleb. She was a history teacher in Vietnam. She and her husband came to the U.S. with their five children. I know she would like to teach again but she thinks it is impossible. I don't think it is. She's really intelligent and her English is quite good.

5   Well, there are 42 other students that I could tell you about but that could take pages and pages. I'll just stop here. I hope you enjoy my book.

Sincerely,
Roni Lebauer

VOCABULARY

author	*n.*	writer
typical	*adj.*	average; usual
technique	*n.*	way of doing something
semester	*n.*	a period of time dividing the school year (such as fall or spring semester)

UNDERSTANDING

1. Look at the picture of Roni's class again. Can you circle Ana Maria? Abu Taleb? Linh? What do you know about each of those students? Write your answers in the chart. (If there is no information, don't write anything.)

Information	Ana Maria	Abu Taleb	Linh
Age			
Previous (Past) Work			
Hopes			

2. This letter is mostly about
   ____ a. Roni's home life
   ____ b. Roni's classes and students
   ____ c. college life in California
   ____ d. college students in California

3. Paragraph 3 is about
   ____ a. how Roni teaches
   ____ b. why Roni teaches
   ____ c. how Roni remembers names
   ____ d. why Roni can't remember names

VOCABULARY PRACTICE: DESCRIBING PEOPLE

You can describe people in many ways. For example, you can give information about their appearance, their personality, their job, or their nationality.

| Goldie Hawn | Pete Sampras | Ella Fitzgerald | Michael Chang | Rosie O'Donnell | Luciano Pavarotti | Billie Holiday |

In the dialogues that follow, people are having problems remembering names. Can you help them?

Do you remember Wimbledon 1994? Who was the guy who won the men's matches? He was American — clean shaven, curly dark hair. What a powerful serve he had! And he was in great shape!

I'm learning about opera and I just bought this tape of Jose Carreras, Placido Domingo and...and...and. Oh, what's the name of the other one — you know — the really famous one — with the moustache and the beard?

What about this video? It has that comedian... you know the one who was in that movie about a woman's baseball team. She's funny. Reddish brown hair. A little heavy. What's her name?

I love old-time jazz and blues singers.

Oh, like Bessie Smith and... oh, what's her name...the one who always wore a flower in her hair?

Ivanasevic? No, the other guy. Oh, yes, it was _____. He played really well.

Oh, _____. How could you forget him?

You mean _____, right?

_____?

Yeah, that's the one!

READING 1.2

On the first day of class, Roni's students fill out forms and give information about themselves.

Name ___Claude Ansari___   Country of Origin ___France___
Native Language ___Arabic___   Time in U.S. ___10 months___   Age: ___25___

Please tell me a little about yourself.

Family: ___I live with my wife and 2-year-old daughter.___

Work: ___I was a medical school student in France but I quit. Now, I'm working as a cook.___

Interests: ___I love to cook (and eat). I also like to go mountain climbing.___

Name ___Su Chen Wang___   Country of Origin ___Taiwan___
Native Language ___Chinese___   Time in U.S. ___4 yrs.___   Age: ___45___

Please tell me a little about yourself.

Family: ___I have 3 boys and 2 girls. They're all attending school here. My husband is a businessman & lives in Taiwan.___

Work: ___I was a math teacher but now I'm a housewife.___

Interests: ___I like indoor activities: reading, listening to music, sewing.___

Name ___Norma Ruiz___   Country of Origin ___Guatemala___
Native Language ___Spanish___   Time in U.S. ___2 yrs.___   Age: ___32___

Please tell me a little about yourself.

Family: ___My family-- my mother and 4 brothers-- lives in Guatemala. I'm here by myself.___

Work: ___I worked as a receptionist in my country. Here I'm a tailor.___

Interests: ___I like to go to movies and rent videos. I love to study.___

SCANNING

How many questions can you answer in two minutes? Write *T* if the sentence is true; write *F* if the sentence is false.

___ 1. Norma is from Mexico.

___ 2. Claude is married.

___ 3. Su Chen likes to play sports.

___ 4. Norma is 25 years old.

___ 5. Claude was a doctor in France.

___ 6. Norma's family is with her in the U.S.

___ 7. Su Chen has three children.

___ 8. Claude's native language is Arabic.

___ 9. Su Chen was a math teacher in Taiwan.

___ 10. Norma and Claude both like to go to movies.

___ 11. Claude arrived in the U.S. less than one year ago.

___ 12. Su Chen is a math teacher now.

___ 13. Su Chen's husband lives in the U.S.

___ 14. Norma was a teacher in Guatemala.

___ 15. Su Chen is in her 50s.

DO IT

Fill in the information form about yourself.

Name _____ Country of Origin _____

Native Language _____ Age: _____

Please tell me a little about yourself.

Family: _____

_____

Work: _____

_____

Interests: _____

_____

Read five of your classmates' forms. How much can you remember 10 minutes later?

5

BEFORE READING 1.3

Look at the title and the picture. What do you think this article will be about? Check (√) your answer.

_____ A special person
_____ How to remember names
_____ Why people forget things
_____ How to choose a name for your child

READING 1.3

I'll Never Forget...What's-His-Name

Joe?...James?...Jack?

1   **D**oes this ever happen to you? Someone introduces you to a friend, you hear his or her name, and then two minutes later, you forget it. Or you go to the same restaurant every day and the owner always says "hello" to you but you can never remember her name. If this happens, you are typical. Most people have some problems remembering names.

2   There are some techniques that can help people remember names. Here are a few of them.
   • Repeat the person's name out loud at least three times while you talk together. For example, instead of saying, "Nice to meet you," say "Nice to meet you, Jack, (or Sue or whatever the person's name is). Instead of saying, "Where do you live?" you can say "Where do you live, Jack?"
   • Introduce the person by name to someone else right away.
   • Write the name down (with a little information about the person) as soon as possible.

3   There are other techniques which may seem a little odd. However, try them. They may work for you.
   • Think of a story using the person's name. For example, think to yourself, "Jack has a nice jacket." Imagine Jack in a nice jacket.
   • Think of a rhyme for the person's name. For example, think to yourself, "Jack would look nice in black." Imagine Jack wearing black clothes.

4   All these techniques have one thing in common. You must pay attention to the people you meet. You can't just meet someone, nod your head, say hello, and walk away. Remembering names takes work and practice.

VOCABULARY

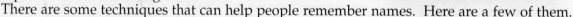

instead of	*prep.*	in place of
odd	*adj.*	unusual
rhyme	*n.*	a word that ends with the same sound as another word (example: house/mouse)
to imagine	*v.*	to create a picture in your thoughts
to have something in common	*v.*	to be the same in certain ways
to pay attention to	*v.*	to listen and watch carefully
to nod	*v.*	to move one's head up and down

1. Look back at your guess on page 6. Were you correct?

2. This article has an introduction, a body, and a conclusion. The introduction here tries to get you interested in the article. The body tells about the main ideas of the article. The conclusion tries to bring everything to a final note.
Paragraph 1 is the

   _____ a. introduction   _____ b. body   _____ c. conclusion

3. The last paragraph is the _____ a. introduction _____ b. body _____ c. conclusion

4. The body of this article gives a list of 5 different

   _____ a. reasons for forgetting names   _____ c. examples of people forgetting names

   _____ b. ways to remember names

5. Your new friend's name is Sue. Write a story or rhyme that could help you remember her name.

   _____

   _____

6. If you want to remember names better, what must you do?

   _____ a. nod your head when you meet people   _____ c. pay attention to people you meet

   _____ b. make sure to say "hello" when you meet people   _____ d. find a rhyme for everyone's name

LOOKING AT LANGUAGE

1. Look at the word that is circled. What is its reference? Draw an arrow to the word or words.

   Example: Where does your father work? (He) works downtown.

   a. You go to the same restaurant every day and the owner always says "hello" to you, but you can never remember (her) name.

   b. You go to the same restaurant every day and the owner always says "hello" to you, but you can never remember her name. If (this) happens, you are typical.

   c. There are some techniques that can help people remember names. Here are a few of (them).

   d. There are other techniques which may seem a little odd. However, try them. (They) may work for you.

2. Finish these sentences with your own ideas.

   a. My best friend and I have many things in common. We both _____.

   b. Instead of eating at home today, let's _____.

   c. When I am in class, I pay attention to _____.

 **CHALLENGE**

The Adams family has 5 children between the ages of 4 and 13. (One is 4; another is 13.) Each child is a different age. Can you figure out the names of the children, their ages, their hair color and type, and their eye color using the information below?

1. The oldest child, Joe, has the same hair color as his sister, Karen. However, one has curly hair; the other has straight hair.
2. The oldest two children are boys — Joe and Jim; the others are girls.
3. Everyone except the four-year-old has brown eyes.
4. The 11-year-old girl, Lena, has the same hair color and type as the 4-year-old.
5. Karen is half (1/2) the age of Jim.
6. Susie, the child with green eyes, has wavy, blonde hair.
7. One of the girls has curly, light brown hair.
8. One of the boys has curly, red hair.

If you think you know the answer, fill in the blanks below.

	Name	Age	Hair Type (straight, wavy, curly)	Hair Color	Eye Color
1.					
2.					
3.					
4.					
5.					

QUOTES AND SAYINGS ABOUT APPEARANCES	• *Appearances are deceiving.* • *Don't judge a book by its cover.*

Which of the following sports did you do when you were younger? Which ones do you do now? Which ones would you like to do in the future? Check (√) "past," "present," or "future" to show your answers. You can check more than one answer for each sport.

Past	Present	Future

Past	Present	Future

Are there other sports that you did when you were younger, that you do now, or that you would like to do? Draw pictures of them in the boxes below.

Past   Present   Future

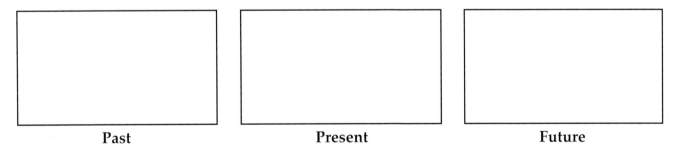

Talk to a classmate and ask these questions:

On a scale of 1 to 4, how athletic were you when you were younger?

1 NOT ATHLETIC AT ALL   4 VERY ATHLETIC

On a scale of 1 to 4, how athletic are you now?

1 NOT ATHLETIC AT ALL   4 VERY ATHLETIC

What sports did you play when you were younger?
What sports do you play now?
What sports would you like to play in the future?

READING 2.1

Friday October

The Herald

Survey: Is it important for children to play sports?

Liz Chance Elementary School Teacher	**Paul Gill** Student	**Lisa Hull** Student	**Masa Takano** Businessman	**Maria Leon** Architect	**Carlos Reyes** Mechanic
"*Absolutely important. I think it is important to raise well-rounded children... not just children who are good at math or science. A healthy body is as important as a healthy mind. And, by the way, I think this is true for boys and girls equally.*"	"*I don't know. Everyone's different. Some people like sports and are good at it. Others prefer more mental activities — reading, listening to music, playing with computers. I think it depends on the kid. Sports are not for everyone. I remember how bad I felt when I was younger when nobody wanted to be on my team. I was never very good at sports.*"	"*Growing up, I didn't have an easy life. My parents fought a lot and I lived in a city with crime and gang problems. I think sports saved my life. Instead of getting into trouble, I played sports. It raised my self-esteem because I knew I played well.*"	"*I think sports are good...but are they really important? I think there are much more important things for children to do — study, learn about the world, travel. When I was younger, I spent hours every day playing tennis. I had a great time but I also didn't get into the university later.*"	"*I think sports teach some good lessons but they also teach some bad lessons. On the good side, children can learn to cooperate with others on a team. Later in life, they may work better with others. But, on the bad side, kids sometimes become too competitive. They think winning is the most important thing.*"	"*I think sports teach kids important lessons about life. It teaches them that sometimes you win and sometimes you lose. You can't win them all. You can't always be the best but you can try. Everyone needs to learn these lessons and participation in sports is a good way to teach them.*"

YOUR TURN

What about you? Who do you agree with? Do you think it is important for children to play sports? Why or why not?

_____

_____

UNDERSTANDING

1. Put a check (√) in the correct box or boxes.

Questions	Liz	Paul	Lisa	Masa	Maria	Carlos
a. Who feels strongly that sports are important for all children?						
b. Who did not enjoy sports when he or she was younger?						
c. Who enjoyed sports when they were younger?						
d. Who thinks that sports can teach kids about life?						

2. The people in the survey give many reasons why sports are or aren't important for children. Look at the reasons below. Check the sentences which give reasons why sports are good.

_____ a. Children may feel bad if nobody wants them on their team.

_____ b. It is important for children to be well-rounded physically and mentally.

_____ c. It gives children something to do instead of getting into trouble.

_____ d. It takes children away from more important things.

_____ e. It teaches children important life lessons.

_____ f. It can raise a child's self-esteem.

_____ g. It teaches children to cooperate with others.

_____ h. It teaches children that winning is the most important thing.

VOCABULARY PRACTICE: SPORTS AND RECREATION

Look at the words in the box. People do some of these activities in water; they do some on ice and in snow. Put the words in the correct category.

Water Activities   Snow/Ice Activities

_____   _____

_____   _____

_____   _____

_____

downhill skiing	rowing
surfing	skating
sailing	sledding
scuba diving	swimming

Are there other sports or recreation activities you can do in the water?

_____

Are there other sports or recreation activities you can do in the snow or on ice?

_____

READING 2.2

Sometimes children, teens and adults want to learn a new sport. One way to learn is to take lessons or classes. Read about some available classes.

ICE SKATING

Introduction to ice skating. Skate rental and free practice time on lesson days included. Please bring a warm jacket, gloves, and socks. Arrive at least 15 minutes prior to lesson. Classes begin the week of June 28 and meet for five weeks. For more information, call Ice Palace at 765-4900.

Ages 3 to 5	# 1267	Tu	1:30-2:00 p.m.
	# 1268	Th	1:30-2:00 p.m.
Ages 6 to 8	# 1269	Tu	4:00-4:30 p.m.
	# 1270	W	6:00-6:30 p.m.
Ages 9 to 15	# 1271	Tu	6:00-6:30 p.m.
	# 1272	Sa	10:30-11:00 a.m.
Adults	# 1273	W	7:30-8:00 p.m.

INTRO TO ICE HOCKEY

Learn the ice skating skills you need to play hockey! First time skaters are welcome. No equipment is needed. Skate rental and free practice time on lesson days from 3 to 5 p.m. included. Wear warm clothes and arrive 30 minutes early. Classes begin the week of June 28 and meet for 6 weeks. For more information, call Ice Palace at 765-4900.

Ages 3-5	# 1274	W	2:00-2:30 p.m.
Ages 6-8	# 1275	W	2:30-3:00 p.m.
Ages 9-15	# 1276	Th	2:30-3:00 p.m.
	# 1277	Th	5:00-5:30 p.m.

SCUBA

mask

snorkel

Over 45 hours of instruction will teach skills of safe SCUBA diving. Course includes six lectures, four pool dives, and five ocean dives. Open to ages 14 and up. The registration fee includes all instruction, books, and use of SCUBA equipment. Students must bring their own mask, snorkel, and fins. Classes begin every Saturday during July and August. For more information, call Joe's Dive School at 677-2894.

fins

VOCABULARY

introduction	*n.*	the beginning lessons
to rent	*v.*	to pay to use something, instead of buying it
prior to	*prep.*	before
equipment	*n.*	the things you need for an activity
lecture	*n.*	a talk or a speech used to teach something
instruction	*n.*	teaching
fee	*n.*	the money you pay for a service

SCANNING

How many can you answer in 2 minutes? Write *T* if the sentence is true ; write *F* if the sentence is false.

45 1:30 – 2:00 1:15   1273   4 – 4:30

___ 1. Ice hockey classes begin the week of June 8.

___ 2. Call 677-2894 if you want more information about SCUBA diving classes.

___ 3. The ice skating class for adults is on Tuesdays.

___ 4. The ice hockey class for 8-year-old kids is on Wednesdays from 2:00 to 2:30.

___ 5. A 14-year-old can take the SCUBA diving class.

___ 6. The class number for the adult ice skating class is #1273.

___ 7. You should arrive at the Ice Palace at 1:45 if your ice hockey class begins at 2:00.

___ 8. You should arrive at the Ice Palace at 1:15 if your ice skating class begins at 1:30.

___ 9. SCUBA diving classes begin every Saturday during July and August.

___ 10. A 4-year-old who wants to play ice hockey can go to class on Tuesday or Thursday.

___ 11. A 4-year-old who wants to go ice skating can go to class on Tuesday or Thursday.

___ 12. The SCUBA class includes more than 45 hours of instruction.

___ 13. Call 765-4500 if you want to learn more about the ice hockey classes.

___ 14. Five classes meet on Thursdays.

___ 15. The ice hockey classes meet for five weeks.

UNDERSTANDING

Fill in the blank with information from Reading 2.2.

1. Ice skating students must take a _____, _____, and _____ to class.

2. SCUBA diving students must take a _____, _____, and _____ to class.

3. How many dives will SCUBA diving students have during the class? _____

4. Ice hockey students do not need to pay for _____ or_____.

5. Ice hockey students should arrive _____ prior to the class.

THINK ABOUT IT

Which activity would you enjoy most: ice skating lessons, ice hockey lessons, or SCUBA diving lessons? Which would you enjoy least?

BEFORE READING 2.3

Do you know who Martina Navratilova is? Work with your classmates and write anything you know about her.

_____

_____

Look at the title. What do you think this article will be about?

_____ Martina Navratilova's tennis career

_____ Martina Navratilova's life away from tennis

_____ Martina Navratilova's tennis career and her life away from tennis

READING 2.3

Martina Navratilova:
On and Off the Tennis Court

1   ***T**ime* magazine called her "the most successful woman in the history of professional sports," and "the most successful tennis player in history." She has earned millions and millions of dollars in her sports career. But there is more to know about Martina Navratilova than tennis and numbers.

2   She grew up in Czechoslovakia*, first in a skiing center in the Krkonose Mountains and then in Revnice, a small town of only 5,000 people. Her family was athletic. Her mother, her stepfather, and her grandmother were all skillful tennis players. No one was surprised that Martina also loved sports. Her childhood was busy — practicing tennis, going to school. Martina jokes that she first got into shape by running to catch the train to Prague (where George Parma, her first professional coach, lived and worked).

3   One of the hardest decisions she ever made was in 1975. After playing in the U.S. Open Game, Navratilova decided not to return to Czechoslovakia. She wanted to stay in the U.S. and the U.S. government gave her permission. This was a painful choice for her. For many years, she couldn't see her family or friends who stayed in Czechoslovakia. She was a woman without a country. (Six years later, she became an American citizen.)

4   She spends her time in different ways. She loves all kinds of sports and physical activities. She skis, plays basketball and golf. She lifts weights and runs to stay in shape. She also enjoys things that people don't expect — mushroom hunting, for example, and designing clothes (sportswear, of course) for women.

5   Navratilova said that 1994, her 22nd year in professional tennis, was her last. "I'm looking forward to living a normal life," she said. Part of her new normal life includes being a mystery book author and writing about a woman detective who is also...yes...a tennis coach!

* now known as the Czech Republic

VOCABULARY

to earn	*v.*	to work and make money
to joke	*v.*	to say something funny
to get into shape	*v.*	to exercise so that you can be in good physical condition
coach	*n.*	a person who teaches athletes to improve their games
decision	*n.*	to come to an answer after thinking about possible choices
detective	*n.*	person whose job is to find answers to mysteries or crimes

AFTER READING 2.3

1. Look at your guess on page 14. Were you correct?

2. Draw a line and match the main idea with the paragraph number.

Paragraph 2   Martina's decision to leave Czechoslovakia

Paragraph 3   Martina's childhood

Paragraph 4   Martina's interests and activities away from the tennis courts

3. Write *T* if the sentence is true; write *F* if the sentence is false.

_____ a. Martina was interested in sports when she was a child.

_____ b. Martina grew up in a large city.

_____ c. Martina is a Czech citizen now.

_____ d. Martina spends all her free time playing sports.

4. Which pictures show Martina's interests? Check (√) the box or boxes.

LOOKING AT LANGUAGE

Sometimes when you read, you will not know a word. What can you do? Sometimes, you can guess the meaning of the word. Try guessing the meaning of the underlined words. Think about what idea fits in that sentence. Match the sentence with the definition.

____ 1. Navratilova decided not to return to Czechoslovakia. She wanted to stay in the U.S. and the U.S. government <u>gave her permission</u>... (Six years later, she became an American citizen.)

    a. able to do something well

____ 2. Martina Navratilova: On and Off the Tennis <u>Court</u>

    b. describing something that hurts and feels bad

____ 3. This was a <u>painful</u> choice for her. For many years, she couldn't see her family or friends who stayed in Czechoslovakia. She was a woman without a country.

    c. to allow someone to do something; to say something is OK to do

____ 4. Her family was athletic. Her mother, her stepfather, and her grandmother were all <u>skillful</u> tennis players.

    d. a place where someone plays a sport (e.g., tennis, basketball, volleyball)

CHALLENGE

All of the words in the crossword puzzle are in Unit 2. Can you complete the crossword puzzle?

Across Clues

6. To play volleyball, you don't need much _____ — just a ball and a net.
8. If you want to go ice skating, you should _____ a warm jacket.
9. She is in good _____ because she exercises and eats right.
11. Martina Navratilova is a famous _____ player.
13. A _____ is someone who helps an athlete play better.

Down Clues

1. Where do you want to play tennis? Let's play at the tennis _____ in the park.
2. You can _____ skis if you don't have them and you don't want to buy them.
3. If you want to take a class, you must pay a registration _____.
4. She was always _____ so she could play every sport well.
5. Tennis, soccer, basketball are the names of _____.
7. Studying is a mental activity; playing sports is a _____ activity.
8. You can't _____ every time. Sometimes, you must lose.
10. The opposite of "win" is _____.
12. Reading is _____ a sport.

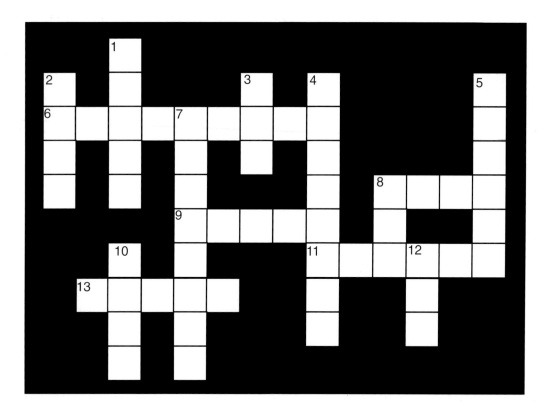

QUOTES AND SAYINGS ABOUT WINNING AND LOSING

• *It's not whether you win or lose; it's how you play the game.*

• *If at first you don't succeed, try, try again.*

What do you do when you have a cold? Check (√) your answers.

"I go to the doctor."

"I stay in bed."

"I take medicine."

"I drink lots of juice."

"I drink lots of hot tea."

"I eat lots of soup."

"I get exercise."

Are there other things you do? Draw pictures and write about other things you do when you have a cold.

Talk to a classmate and ask these questions:

How often do you get colds?
What do you do when you get a cold?
How often do you go to a doctor?
Last year, did you need to go to a doctor? Why?

17

READING 3.1

A get well message for you

Dear Marta,

I'm sending my best with this little card. Get well my friend!

Best Wishes,
Roni

Dear Marta,

I can't believe you're home sick again. You seem to be getting a lot of colds this year. What are you doing to take care of yourself?

I don't know about you but when I'm sick with a cold, I always make some chicken soup. I follow my grandmother's recipe. I can't say why it works but it does. I'm attaching the recipe--maybe it will work for you, too. (Why don't you try it?)

Don't worry about missing class. When you return, I'll help you catch up to the other students.

Just rest and don't worry.
Get well soon!

Best wishes,
Roni

ANNA LEBAUER'S CHICKEN SOUP

1 INGREDIENTS:
   • ONE MEDIUM-SIZED CHICKEN
   • TWO ONIONS, CHOPPED
   • 10 CARROTS, SLICED
   • 5 STALKS OF CELERY, CHOPPED
   • SALT AND PEPPER

2 CUT CHICKEN INTO ABOUT 6 PIECES. CLEAN THE CHICKEN. DON'T REMOVE THE SKIN. PUT THE CHICKEN IN A LARGE POT WITH WATER AND ONIONS. BRING TO A BOIL. COOK, UNCOVERED, OVER MEDIUM HEAT FOR ONE HALF HOUR. ADD REMAINING INGREDIENTS, COVER AND COOK OVER LOW HEAT ONE HOUR LONGER OR UNTIL CARROTS AND CHICKEN ARE TENDER. THE SOUP IS READY.

3 (FOR A HEALTHIER SOUP, PUT THE SOUP IN THE REFRIGERATOR. WHEN THE SOUP COOLS, REMOVE THE FAT THAT RISES TO THE TOP. THEN, REHEAT THE SOUP — WITHOUT THE FAT!)

VOCABULARY

recipe	n.	directions for cooking something
to catch up	v.	to get to the same point as others (after being behind)
ingredients	n.	food necessary to make a dish
to chop	v.	to cut into small pieces
to slice	v.	to cut into thin, flat pieces
to boil	v.	to bring water to 212° Fahrenheit (100° Celsius)
tender	adj.	soft

UNDERSTANDING

1. Marta is ____ **a.** a teacher. ____ **b.** a student. ____ **c.** a doctor.

2. Marta ____ gets colds. ____ **a.** never ____ **b.** often ____ **c.** rarely

3. What 3 suggestions does Roni give Marta for getting well? Write them in the blank.

   She tells her to _____ and _____. She tells her not to _____.

4. Which of the following are necessary to make Anna Lebauer's chicken soup?
   Check (√) your answers.

5. How long does it take to make Anna Lebauer's chicken soup?
   Check (√) your answer.

   ___ **a.** less than one hour ___ **b.** between one and two hours ___ **c.** between two and three hours

6. Number the pictures below to show how to make Anna Lebauer's chicken soup.
   Write *1* for the first step, *2* for the second step, and so on.

VOCABULARY PRACTICE: HEALTH PROBLEMS AND REMEDIES

Make sentences with the words below, using the form, "*When you have _____ , you should _____ .*"

Example: *When you have <u>a sore throat</u> , you should drink <u>hot liquids</u>.*

You can add your own remedies.

Health Problems	Remedies
a backache	rest
a headache	see a doctor
a fever	drink hot liquids
the hiccups	use an ice pack
chest pain	use a heating pad
a cough	take aspirin or medicine
the flu	take cough syrup
	take vitamins
	hold your breath and swallow

READING 3.2

Marta went to the store to buy some cold medicine. (Perhaps she didn't try Anna Lebauer's chicken soup remedy!) She found the following box of medicine.

Here is the front of the box:

DIMAFED
Severe Cold Medicine

Fast Relief For: • *Nasal and Sinus Congestion* • *Coughing* • *Body Aches and Pains*
• *Minor Sore Throat Pain* • *Headache* • *Fever*

NO DROWSINESS!   10 Capsules

Here is the back of the box:

Directions and Dosage
Adults and children 12 years of age and over: Take 2 capsules every 6 hours with water, not to exceed 8 capsules in 24 hours.
Not recommended for children under 12 years of age.
Warnings
• Do not exceed recommended dosage. At higher doses, dizziness or sleeplessness may occur.
• Do not take this product for more than 10 days. A persistent cough may be a sign of a serious condition. If cough persists for more than 8 days, consult a physician.
• If sore throat is severe or persists for more than 2 days, consult a physician.
• Do not take this medicine if you have high blood pressure or heart disease.
• If you are pregnant or nursing a baby, consult a physician before taking this medicine.

KEEP THIS DRUG OUT OF REACH OF CHILDREN

VOCABULARY

| Sinus congestion | dizzy | measuring blood pressure | a pregnant woman | a mother nursing a baby |

severe	*adj.*	serious; not mild
relief	*n.*	the good feeling at the end of pain or trouble
nasal congestion	*n.*	a health problem when air cannot enter or exit easily through the nose
minor	*adj.*	not serious; not very important
drowsiness	*n.*	sleepiness
dosage/dose	*n.*	how often and how much you should take of a medicine
to exceed	*v.*	to be more than
to persist	*v.*	to stay for a long time
warning	*n.*	a statement telling something you should be careful about
to consult	*v.*	talk to; get the advice from
physician	*n.*	a doctor

SCANNING

How fast can you answer these questions?

1. How many capsules are in the box of medicine? _____

2. You should not take this medicine if you are under what age? _____

3. How many capsules should you take every six hours? _____

UNDERSTANDING

1. **Make a complete sentence by matching ideas on the left with ideas on the right.**

   a. If you are pregnant,   _____ do not take this medicine.

   b. If you have heart disease,   _____ talk to a doctor before taking this medicine.

   c. If you take more than   _____ you may get dizzy and you may not be
   the recommended dosage,   able to sleep.

2. **Write *T* if the sentence is true; write *F* if the sentence is false. If the sentence is false, correct it.**

   _____ a. If you take the recommended dosage, this medicine will make you sleepy.

   _____ b. If you take more than the recommended dosage, this medicine will make you dizzy.

   _____ c. Children under 12 can take 1/2 the dosage of adults.

   _____ d. This medicine is for severe sore throats.

   _____ e. You can take this medicine as long as you want.

   _____ f. Adults should not take more than 2 capsules in 24 hours.

THINK ABOUT IT

On the back of the box, it says "KEEP THIS DRUG OUT OF THE REACH OF CHILDREN." Why is this in capital letters? In your house, where is the medicine? Is it out of reach of children?

BEFORE READING 3.3

This article is about soups that people eat when they are sick. The article says that in most parts of the world, people give soup to sick people. Of course, the recipes are different. Tell the class about soups that you make or your parents make when family members are sick.

READING 3.3

Take Two Bowls and Call Me in the Morning

1   Some like it spicy. Some like it bland. Some like it with rice. Some like it with noodles. Some put yogurt in it. Some put lemon or lime in it. However people make it, they agree about one thing: soup is good for a cold. Why is that?

2   There are a few reasons. For one thing, a sick person needs nutritious food and liquids. A chicken or meat or vegetable broth provides both. In addition, a sick person may have difficulty swallowing and digesting food. Broth is easy to swallow and digest. Lastly, the vapor rising from hot soup can relieve nasal congestion.

3   In Nigeria, there is a type of soup called "nsala." May Ndubuisi, a restaurant owner and Nigerian cook, says "everybody in Nigeria knows what you mean if you call it pepper soup. It's the very richest soup we make, with several kinds of meat in it — fresh fish, dried fish, smoked fish, chicken, meat — so it's very nutritious and it's also full of medicinal herbs and spices. The herbs are good for you and the hot pepper opens up your nasal passages so you breathe well." Hot pepper is popular in many soup recipes from Asia and Mexico also.

4   In many countries, cooks use ginger in their soup remedies. Prem Chadda, a restaurant owner and Indian cook, says "ginger opens all the passages. At my restaurant, all the workers get this kind of soup when they have a cold, even the non-Indians."

5   A Filipino dish, "arroz caldo," includes it all: a chicken broth with rice, red pepper <u>and</u> ginger. (They throw some garlic in the pot, too, just for a little more help in getting better!)

6   Next time you think about calling a physician or going to the pharmacy or drugstore for a cold medicine, think again. Perhaps a remedy is in your refrigerator!

VOCABULARY

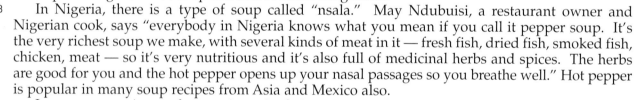

vapor

spicy	*adj.*	containing or tasting like spices
bland	*adj.*	without much taste; without spices
nutritious	*adj.*	healthy; full of vitamins
broth	*n.*	the soup that comes from boiling vegetables or meat or chicken or fish
to swallow	*v.*	to move food or liquid from the mouth down the throat
to digest	*v.*	to move food or liquid through the body, in and out of the stomach
to relieve	*v.*	to cause relief; to feel good after feeling pain or trouble
herbs and spices	*n.*	different kinds of plants which are used to make medicine or improve the taste of food
to breathe	*v.*	to take air in and out
remedy	*n.*	a cure; something that can make a sick person better

1. **This article is about**

   ___ where you can find the best soup.

   ___ why different soups are good for colds.

   ___ why it is not good to go to doctors.

2. **There are 6 paragraphs in this article.**

   a. Which paragraph is the introduction?   Paragraph # _____

   b. Which paragraph gives reasons why soup is good for a cold?   Paragraph # _____

   c. Which paragraphs give examples of different kinds of healthy soups?

      Paragraphs # _____ ,   # _____ ,   and # _____

   d. Which paragraph is a conclusion?   Paragraph # _____

3. **Look at paragraph 2. This paragraph tells you three reasons why soup is good for a cold. What are those three reasons?**

   a. _____   b. _____   c. _____

4. **In paragraph 2, the words "for one thing" tell you that one reason will follow. The words "in addition" tell you another reason will follow. What other word in paragraph 2 tells you that one more reason will follow?** _____

LOOKING AT LANGUAGE

1. **Sometimes when you don't know a word, you look it up in the dictionary. Look at this definition for the word "rich." Notice that there are four different definitions for the word.**

   rich / ritʃ / *adj.* **1** (of a person) wealthy; having a lot of money or things **2** (of food) containing a lot of cream, sugar, eggs, etc.: *a rich cake* **3** (of land) good for growing plants in: *rich land* **4** (of a sound or color) deep and strong: *a rich dark blue*

   In the article, the Nigerian woman says "it's the richest soup we make." Which definition fits this sentence?   Definition # _____

   Read each sentence below and write the number of the definition that fits the sentence.

   a. She is a rich woman because she owns a lot of houses.   Definition # _____

   b. The piano has a rich sound.   Definition # _____

   c. What a rich cake! We're going to get fat.   Definition # _____

2. **Look at the word that is circled. What is its reference? Draw an arrow to the word or words.**

   Example: I always eat soup when I'm sick. (It) makes me feel better.

   a. A sick person needs nutritious food and liquids. A chicken broth provides (both.)

   b. All the workers get this kind of soup when (they) have a cold.

 CHALLENGE

Can you find 20 words related to health in this puzzle? You may find the words vertically (↕), horizontally (↔), or diagonally (↗) or (↘). The word list is below.

capsule	doctor	headache	medicine
cold	dose	pain	nurse
congestion	drowsy	pharmacy	nutritious
cough	drug	physician	remedy
dizzy	fever	pregnant	wheelchair

P	H	A	R	C	A	P	S	C	W	I	N	D
N	P	I	Z	Z	Y	H	A	O	H	O	M	E
C	U	H	E	A	D	A	C	H	E	L	E	N
O	O	R	Y	H	P	R	D	O	E	N	D	P
N	D	U	S	S	A	M	R	S	L	A	I	H
G	R	O	G	E	I	A	O	N	C	D	C	Y
E	T	H	S	H	N	C	W	O	H	I	I	S
S	R	E	M	E	D	Y	S	D	A	Z	N	I
T	D	F	A	I	Y	Z	Y	A	I	Z	E	C
I	P	R	E	G	N	A	N	T	R	Y	A	I
O	R	R	U	V	C	A	P	S	U	L	E	A
N	C	L	O	G	E	D	O	C	T	O	R	N
E	D	O	N	U	T	R	I	T	I	O	U	S

QUOTES AND SAYINGS ABOUT HEALTH	• *Laughter is the best medicine.* • *There is a remedy for everything except death.*

Where do you usually eat lunch? Check (√) the picture or pictures.

"I eat at home."

"I buy food from a vendor."

"I go to a fast food restaurant."

"I go to a fancy restaurant."

"I eat at a neighborhood restaurant."

"I eat at a cafeteria."

"I eat at my desk at work."

"I order take-out or home delivered foods."

Talk to a classmate and ask these questions:

Do you prefer to eat at home or eat out?

How often do you eat out?

How often do you eat at fancy restaurants?

How often do you eat at fast food restaurants?

Do you buy food from street vendors? If so, what do you buy?

READING 4.1

Saturday, April

The Herald

Survey: What's your favorite restaurant and why?

Lola Lopez Actress	**Hiro Yamada** Businessman	**Jim Janssen** High School Student	**Maria Luig** University Student	**Gina Mangino** Housewife	**Raul Sanchez** Pharmacist

"There's a tiny French restaurant near my apartment. It's my favorite. The service is great. The food is always cooked well and served beautifully. And the atmosphere is very romantic... candles, low lights, white tablecloths. It's a little expensive but it's worth it... and I'm worth it!"

"When I need to take customers out for business lunches or dinners, I always choose The Steak House. It's a very comfortable restaurant and the specialty is steak. The food is always excellent, and the service is great. It's also good because they never rush you out of the restaurant. If I have an important customer to meet with, I don't want to feel rushed."

"I'm hooked on fast foods. Chicken, burgers, fish, tacos, french fries—I love it all. My mom says I should eat healthier foods but it tastes so good! Also, I'm not rich and the price of fast food is just right for me. Oh...one more thing! You don't need to dress up to go to a fast food restaurant. Who wants to wear a suit and tie to eat ???"

"My favorite restaurant is Rosie's Restaurant. It's just a cheap, little "hole-in-the-wall" restaurant. Nothing fancy — just some tables, chairs, a few pictures on the walls. But Rosie cooks just like my mom does at home. Everything is fresh and tasty. It seems like Rosie cooks everything with love."

"With three kids, I'm not interested in a fancy restaurant with low lights and romantic music. I look for a place that has good food at a reasonable price. I look for a place that's comfortable for children and serves the food quickly because my kids can't sit still for a long time. That's why I like Sam's Chinese restaurant. There's so much on the menu. The kids and I can always find something we like."

"I can't remember the last time I ate out...maybe a year ago. Maybe that's because my wife and I really like to cook. Instead of eating out, we look through a cookbook and find some new recipes. The price is right, the atmosphere is great, the food is cooked just the way we like it. Why would we want to go out??"

YOUR TURN

What about you? What's your favorite restaurant? Why do you like it?

UNDERSTANDING

1. Look at the drawings below. Write the name of the person from page 26 who likes this kind of restaurant.

_____   _____   _____   _____

2. Who doesn't care if a place is expensive?
   ___ **a.** Lola   ___ **b.** Jim   ____ **c.** Gina

3. Who doesn't like to eat out?
   ___ **a.** Gina   ___ **b.** Hiro   ____ **c.** Raul

4. Who likes romantic atmosphere?
   ___ **a.** Gina   ___ **b.** Lola   ____ **c.** Maria

5. Who likes home-cooking?
   ___ **a.** Lola and Hiro   ___ **b.** Gina and Jim   ____ **c.** Maria and Raul

6. Who likes to eat slowly?
   ___ **a.** Jim   ___ **b.** Hiro   ____ **c.** Gina

VOCABULARY PRACTICE: TALKING ABOUT RESTAURANTS

Some of the words in the box can describe a restaurant's atmosphere; some of the words can describe a restaurant's food; some of the words can describe a restaurant's service. Put the words from the box in the correct category. Some words can go in more than one category.

Words Describing Atmosphere	Words Describing Food	Words Describing Service		
			tasty	fast
_____	_____	_____	romantic	fresh
_____	_____	_____	delicious	fancy
_____	_____	_____	comfortable	attentive
_____	_____	_____	noisy	healthy
			slow	polite

READING 4.2

Look at these ads for restaurants.

VOCABULARY

cuisine	*n.*	style of cooking
valet parking	*n.*	a parking service
brunch	*n.*	a meal that is a combination of breakfast and lunch, usually eaten between 11 and 2 on weekends
to hang out	*v.*	to relax and spend time somewhere without hurrying or doing anything special (slang)
cool	*adj.*	stylish; in fashion; up-to-date (slang)

SCANNING

Write *T* if the sentence is true. Write *F* if the sentence is false. You have 2 minutes.

___ 1. Starlight Cafe serves desserts.

___ 2. Rajah Restaurant is open on Mondays.

___ 3. Rajah Restaurant has two locations.

___ 4. Verano Restaurant serves seafood and fish.

___ 5. Rajah Restaurant has valet parking.

___ 6. Verano Restaurant has two phone numbers.

___ 7. Verano Restaurant serves Indian cuisine.

___ 8. No one will rush you at the Starlight Cafe.

___ 9. Rajah Restaurant sometimes has music.

___ 10. Starlight Cafe is open every day of the week.

___ 11. Rajah Restaurant will deliver food to your home.

___ 12. Rajah Restaurant opens every day at 11 a.m.

___ 13. Starlight Cafe is open until 2 a.m. on Saturdays.

___ 14. Verano Restaurant has 3 locations.

___ 15. Starlight Cafe opens at 9:30 a.m. on Saturdays.

THINK ABOUT IT

1. **Rajah Restaurant serves a "2 For 1 Dinner." What does this mean?**
_____

2. **Verano Restaurant's brunch is "All You Can Eat." What does this mean?**
_____

3. **Starlight Cafe's ad has a <u>coupon</u>. What does the coupon say?**
_____

   This means that you get a drink if you order a _____ or _____.
   If you want to get a free drink, what must you take to the restaurant? _____.

TALK ABOUT IT

Talk to a classmate. The two of you are going to eat out together and you are thinking about Rajah Restaurant, Verano Restaurant, or the Starlight Cafe. Talk to your classmate and decide which restaurant you both like. Tell the class your choice and why you chose that restaurant.

BEFORE READING 4.3

Those golden arches are everywhere. There are stores in Paris, in Tokyo, in Kuala Lumpur, in Beijing, in Sao Paolo, in Mexico City, in Moscow, to name a few. There are more than 10,000 restaurants worldwide. On its first day of business in Belgrade, Yugoslavia, the McDonald's served 6,000 people. Seven of the eleven busiest McDonald's restaurants in the world are in Hong Kong. Why is this restaurant so successful? Talk to your classmates and write down your ideas.

WHY AMERICANS EAT AT McDONALD'S	WHY PEOPLE IN OTHER COUNTRIES EAT AT McDONALD'S

Penny Moser wrote an article for a business magazine called <u>Fortune.</u> Part of the article is below. In this part, she gives her opinion about why McDonald's is so popular with Americans, like herself.

READING 4.3

WHY WE KEEP GOING TO McDONALD'S
by Penny Moser

[1] After that first meal in 1957, McDonald's never left my life. Although my family moved, we were never far from Mac's. I remember the whole family, with Grandma or an uncle, remarking when the sign changed...100 million hamburgers sold...200...300...500.

[2] By the time I headed off to college in 1967, the sign said 3 billion. By now, all of America was heading for the golden arches. We were hooked on the taste. Some of us were having kids of our own.

[3] Several factors had been at work over those years to make McDonald's part of our culture. After World War II, America went car crazy. Times were good, and in general, we began to hurry. At McDonald's, we could get out of our parent's car, walk up to the window, and order — a very grown-up thing to do. It was also more fun than having to sit in a restaurant, where there was nothing to do but shake salt on your sister. We learned to hate to wait.

[4] Instead of being bored with McDonald's sameness, we learned to appreciate it. In a world where everything is changing, McDonald's became a symbol of stability. A McDonald's meal tastes pretty much the same everywhere.

[5] I'm a McDonald's stockholder now — a little one, but a stockholder just the same. "No matter what happens," my stockbroker told me, "people are still going to eat at McDonald's." I'm sure I will.

VOCABULARY

meal	n.	breakfast, lunch or dinner
to remark	v.	to say something
to be hooked on something	v.	to have a great liking for something and need to use or do it a lot
factor	n.	things that cause or affect a result
to be car crazy	v.	to be crazy about cars; to be really excited about cars
symbol	n.	a sign or object which makes you think of an idea; for example, a flag is a symbol of a country
stable	adj.	describing something which doesn't change (or changes only a little) over time
stockholder	n.	a person who pays money to own a part of the company (stock)
stockbroker	n.	a person who sells stock in a company to stockholders

AFTER READING 4.3

1. **The author gives a number of reasons why McDonald's became popular with Americans like herself. Put an _R_ (for "Reason") in front of the reasons the author names.**

   ____ a. People liked the taste of the food.

   ____ b. People liked the golden arches.

   ____ c. People wanted cheap food.

   ____ d. People wanted to get their food quickly.

   ____ e. Children felt grown-up when they ordered food for themselves.

   ____ f. Children didn't like to sit in restaurants with nothing to do while they waited.

   ____ g. People liked to buy stocks in McDonald's.

   ____ h. People liked that McDonald's meals taste the same everywhere.

   ____ i. In a world full of changes, people wanted something that didn't change.

2. **In the first paragraph, the author says, "I remember the whole family remarking when the sign changed...100 million sold...200...300...500." What do the numbers refer to?** ____ **a.** stores _____ **b.** people ____ **c.** hamburgers

3. **Read the last paragraph again. The last line is "I'm sure I will." What will the author do?**

   ___ **a.** buy more stock in McDonald's ___ **b.** eat at McDonalds again ___ **c.** stop eating at McDonalds

LOOKING AT LANGUAGE

1. **Try to guess the meaning of the underlined words below. Write your guess.**

   a. "By the time I headed off to college, the sign said 3 billion. By now, all of America was <u>heading</u> for the golden arches." _____

   b. "Instead of being bored with McDonald's sameness, we learned to <u>appreciate</u> it." _____

2. **Look at this sentence from the article.**

   "It was also more fun than having to sit in a restaurant, where there was nothing to do but shake salt on your sister."

   In this sentence, "but" means the same as "except."
   a. Everyone likes McDonald's but Jose. Does Jose like McDonald's? _____
   b. All but two children went to the park. Did everyone go to the park? _____
   c. Laura didn't write anyone but her mother. Did Laura write her mother? _____

THINK ABOUT IT

Penny Moser wrote this article about Americans and for Americans. She expected Americans to read this article. Your experience is probably different. Talk with your classmates about the following:

- In the countries you know well, is McDonald's popular? Why or why not?
- Do you hope more or fewer McDonald's will open there? Why or why not?

CHALLENGE

How much do you know about food? If you can answer 7 or more of these questions, you know quite a bit!

1. Which country produces the most rice?
   ___ **a.** Vietnam   ____ **b.** Indonesia   ____ **c.** China

2. Which country uses the most rice?
   ___ **a.** Iran   ____ **b.** China   ____ **c.** Indonesia

3. Where did rice first come from?
   ___ **a.** Indonesia and Iran   ____ **b.** China and Japan   ____ **c.** India and China

4. Where did tomatoes first come from?
   ____ **a.** the Americas   ____ **b.** Africa   ____ **c.** Europe

5. A cup of which vegetable has the most calories?
   ____ **a.** mushrooms   ____ **b.** onions   ____ **c.** peas

6. What does Vitamin A do?
   ____ **a.** It helps build strong bones.
   ____ **b.** It helps digestion.
   ____ **c.** It is good for eyesight.

7. What food is high in Vitamin A?
   ____ **a.** carrots   ____ **b.** garlic   ____ **c.** mushrooms

8. Which food is <u>not</u> high in Vitamin C?
   ____ **a.** oranges   ____ **b.** potatoes   ____ **c.** lettuce

9. Which country does <u>not</u> grow coffee?
   ____ **a.** the United States   ____ **b.** Costa Rica   ____ **c.** Egypt

10. Which oil is healthiest?
    ____ **a.** coconut oil   ____ **b.** olive oil   ____ **c.** corn oil

---

QUOTES AND SAYINGS ABOUT FOOD

- *A hungry man is not a free man.*

- *Honey catches more flies than vinegar.*

My phone rang, waking me from a deep sleep. "Hello." I tried to sound professional but it was difficult. I heard a woman's voice. "Is this 535-3679? Detective Ann Ryan?"

"Yes, it is." I was beginning to wake up. No more long nights at the office for me, I thought to myself. Work or no work, I need to go home and get a good night's sleep.

"Detective Ryan, can I meet you right away? It's very important. I'd rather not leave my house so I'd appreciate it if you would come to my home. I live near Union Square."

"That's not a problem but first I need to know who this is."

"I'm so sorry. My name is Liz Aaron. I'm a physician. My specialty is neck pain. Oh, that shouldn't matter to you. Please excuse me. You see, I just noticed that my mother's ring is missing and I'm very upset."

"Ms. Aaron, I can be at your house in a half hour. Is that O.K.?"

"That would be wonderful. I'm at 12 Oak Street."

"I know where that is. I'll be there soon."

"Thank you so much. Goodbye."

"Bye."

A quick cup of strong coffee and I was out the door. Rush hour was over so there was no traffic and I got to her house in 20 minutes — 10 minutes early. I rang the bell. No answer. That's strange, I thought. She said she didn't want to leave the house. I rang again. Still no answer. Rather than wait at the front door, I used the time to look around. A small house, one floor, one entrance. At that moment, I looked up and saw a young woman — medium height, a little heavy, with long blonde hair — walking towards me.

"Oh, I'm so sorry. I just stepped out to get some milk. I thought you might like some coffee or tea. I'm Liz Aaron. You must be Detective Ryan."

"Please call me Ann."

"Then you must call me Liz." I followed Liz down a long hall into the dining room where we sat and talked.

"It's a ring," she said, "that means a lot to me. It's not really very valuable. The stones aren't real — just red and green colored glass. Perhaps someone thought they were rubies or emeralds. Truthfully, it's only valuable to me. It was my mother's and before that, her mother's — my grandmother's."

"I understand," I said.

"I never take it off — except to bathe or wash the dishes."

"When did you last see it?"

"I had a dinner party last night. Four guests. I remember putting the ring on before the party and taking it off to wash the dishes after dinner. I probably put it down near the sink. I first noticed it was missing after everyone left. I looked for it in every possible place in the kitchen. I'm sure it's not there."

"Who was in the kitchen with you last night?"

"Everyone except Pat, at one time or another. Sue and Connor helped me serve and Jack helped me clean up. Pat has knee problems so she stayed seated all evening."

"Sue? Jack? Connor? Pat?" I needed more information.

"Sue and Jack Lane are married. Connor's their son. Pat is Jack's mother."

"I'd like to meet with your guests. Would you mind if I called them to set up an interview?"

"Oh no, please don't. I don't want to embarrass them if they didn't take it."

"Ok. I'll need photos, then. One more question. Why don't you go to the police and ask them for help?"

"It's not an expensive ring. They probably won't work too hard on this case. They have more important things to do. And I really want my ring back."

I was ready to leave. Liz stood up and went to a drawer to get me photos of the Lane family. While she was busy, I took a quick look at the kitchen. It was a small and dark room. There was only one door and that led to the dining room.

I left the house not sure where to start. I had an idea about who did it but I needed proof. I decided to go home and take a nap first. I do my best thinking in bed.

Later that afternoon, I called my friend, Carl, a jeweller in the Lanes' neighborhood. He agreed to cooperate with me. Next, I bought an ad in the local newspaper. A simple and cheap one but eye-catching. It just said "Rubies wanted. All sizes. Will pay cash." I gave Carl's number.

The following day, I waited in Carl's store. (I have experience as a salesperson so I helped Carl a little, too.) A number of people came in, but their rubies were real. Carl thanked them but said no. Finally, at 3:00, one of the Lanes came in — with red pieces of glass.

I smiled to myself. That wasn't hard at all.

UNDERSTANDING

Look at the pictures below. Number the pictures from 1-8 to show the events in time.

DO IT

Work in groups of three to read this story out loud to the class. One person is the narrator. One person is the detective. One person is Liz. If you are male, you can change the detective's name to Arnold Ryan and read that part. The narrator can be male or female.

THINK ABOUT IT

Who probably took the ring? (Hints: When and where did Liz take off the ring? When were Sue and Connor in the kitchen? When was Jack in the kitchen? Was Pat in the kitchen?)

UNIT 6 Somewhere in the World

 Work in pairs to match these famous places to their locations on the map.

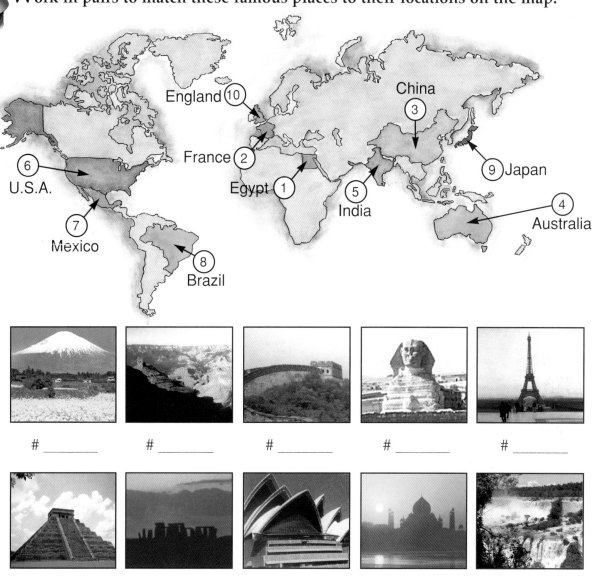

\#_____   \#_____   \#_____   \#_____   \#_____

\#_____   \#_____   \#_____   \#_____   \#_____

Talk to a classmate and ask these questions:

Do you like to travel?
What was your favorite trip?
Where did you go?
When did you go?
Who did you go with?
How long were you there?
What did you see and do on this trip?
Why did you like this trip so much?

READING 6.1

During the summer, Roni's students often send her postcards.

Firenze

Dear Roni,
 Italy is wonderful. We started in Rome 2 weeks ago, drove to Florence last week and now we're on our way to Venice. Three weeks just isn't enough.
 The countryside near Florence is so beautiful-- rolling hills, olive trees. And the red roofs of the houses look so pretty from a distance.
 Love,
 Akemi
P.S. I'm gaining weight--the pasta and desserts are so good!!!

Roni Lebauer
222 Main St.
Laguna Beach, CA
92651
U.S.A.

AIR MAIL

Aloha

Hi Roni,
 I can't believe you went to school here. Why did you leave??
 I spend each morning on the beach and in the water. The sand is so soft and the beaches seem endless. The water is just the right temperature and the waves aren't too rough (at least on this side of the island!)
 One afternoon, I left the beach to hike in the mountains near Honolulu. The path was very muddy and slippery but the view was incredible.
 I wish you were here!

 Mari

Roni Lebauer
222 Main Street
Laguna Beach, CA
92651

Dear Roni,
 Maybe I'm strange but I love the desert! Last week, our group spent 4 days camping in the desert. At times, it felt like the moon!!
 I always thought deserts were all the same! They're not. Some parts are really mountainous; others are very flat. Sometimes the wind creates tall sand dunes.
 And then it feels like magic when we find an oasis-- a few palm trees, a little water. It's great!

 See you in September,
 Kim

AIR MAIL
PAR AVION

Ms. Roni Lebauer
222 Main St.
Laguna Beach CA
92651
U.S.A.

Mysterious Morocco

UNDERSTANDING

1. Check the correct box or boxes.

	Akemi	Mari	Kim	Roni
a. Who is having a good time?				
b. Who went to school in Hawaii?				
c. Who may be traveling by herself?				
d. Who learned something new on his or her trip?				
e. Who slept in a tent?				

2. Write *T* if the sentence is true. Write *F* if the sentence is false.

___ **a.** Akemi is taking public transportation only — buses, trains, etc.
___ **b.** Akemi is staying 2 weeks in Italy.
___ **c.** Akemi likes the food in Italy.
___ **d.** Mari is spending every morning and afternoon at the beach.
___ **e.** In Hawaii, the mountain path was very dry.
___ **f.** In Morocco, the desert always looks the same.
___ **g.** There is no water in the desert in Morocco.

VOCABULARY PRACTICE: PLACES

Look at these pictures. Label them with a word from the box.

rocks
sand dunes
sandy beach
rolling hills
mountains
plains
a desert oasis
a muddy path
big waves
calm water
crowded streets
empty streets

_____ _____

_____ _____ _____ _____

_____ _____ _____ _____

READING 6.2

Some people like to plan their trips by themselves. They like to travel with a friend or family. They don't want to travel with a group of strangers. Other people prefer to travel with a group and a guide. They go to a travel agent and they look at brochures. They choose a trip that sounds good to them.

Look at the trip brochure describing a safari to Tanzania. (A safari is a trip to Africa to see wildlife in their natural location.)

SEE TANZANIA!!
11 DAYS/10 NIGHTS

DAY 1: YOUR HOME TO ARUSHA, TANZANIA.

Fly into Arusha in northern Tanzania. Perhaps you'll get a good view of Mt. Kilimanjaro, the highest mountain in Africa. (It's also an active volcano.) Overnight at a hotel in town.

DAYS 2-4: NGORONGORO CRATER.

We begin with a morning visit to the busy marketplace of Arusha. Then, we head to the forest highlands to visit Ngorongoro Crater. (Don't worry. The volcano died a long time ago!!!) We'll camp three nights on the edge of the crater. Every day, we'll go down into this huge crater to watch the wildlife: lions, rhinos, zebras, and even pink flamingoes.

DAYS 5-7: SERENGETI NATIONAL PARK

We leave the highlands and travel to the plains of the Serengeti for two full days of animal watching. Serengeti National Park, with its endless grasslands, is a great place to see giraffes, lions, and zebras. We'll camp close to the animals — but safely!!

DAY 8: OLDUVAI GORGE/OLDEANI

We travel across the plains and stop at Olduvai Gorge. It was here that the Leakey family of archeologists found a bone — one of the oldest human bones ever found. You can camp near the village of Oldeani or stay in the home of local hosts.

DAYS 9-10: TARANGIRE NATIONAL PARK

You can enjoy two nights in Tarangire National Park, the third largest park in Tanzania. The park includes grasslands, forests, rocky hilltops. In the park, you'll probably see elephants, lions, and many kinds of birds. Camp with the sounds of the animals all around you.

DAY 11: ARUSHA

Return to Arusha and fly home that evening with good memories, addresses of new friends, and lots of photographs.

AFRICA

TANZANIA ★

VOCABULARY

volcano

rhino

flamingoes

lions

giraffes

crater

zebra

bone

elephants

UNDERSTANDING

1. Look at the pictures below. Number them from 1-8 to show the order that you will see these places or animals if you take the Tanzania safari described on page 38.

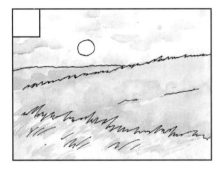  

2. How many nights will you stay in a hotel on this trip? _____
   How many nights will you camp on this trip? _____ or _____
   On Day 8, you can camp or _____.

3. What's the tallest mountain in Africa? _____
   What's the third largest park in Tanzania? _____
   Where did archaeologists find one of the oldest human bones? _____

THINK ABOUT IT

1. On Day 8, travelers have a choice of camping or staying with a local host. Which would you choose? Why?
2. Does this sound like an interesting trip to you? Why or why not?
3. You have a choice: the trip described on page 38 or an 11-day trip to Hawaii's beaches (staying at reasonably-priced hotels). Which would you choose? Why?

 Tell a classmate about your choices.

BEFORE READING 6.3

When you and your classmates hear the word *Hawaii*, what do you imagine? Write a list of things you associate with Hawaii.

_____

_____

READING 6.3

Another Hawaii: The Big Island

1   Say the word *Hawaii* and most people imagine endless beaches, palm trees, mist-covered mountains. Some people associate the word with Honolulu — a busy city of modern skyscrapers and government buildings. Others associate the word with Waikiki Beach, the vacation spot for countless tourists. However, there are other sides to Hawaii that many people never see. Visitors who want to see *another* Hawaii might start at *The Big Island*.

2   If you look at the map, you can see that there are eight major islands of Hawaii. Oahu is the island that most visitors know; it includes Honolulu and Waikiki Beach. The other islands are Maui, Kauai, Molokai, Lanai, Niihau, Kahoolawe, and an island named Hawaii. It is this island named *Hawaii* that most residents call *The Big Island*. (Some people also call it *The Orchid Island* or *The Volcano Island*.)

3   Although people call it *The Big Island*, it's not that big. It's less than 1/3 the size of Taiwan. In fact, more than 700 "Big Islands" can fit into Australia!!!

4   However, within this one island, a traveler can find arid deserts, active and dead volcanoes, black sand beaches, white sand beaches, snow covered mountains, forests, grasslands, valleys, rivers, streams, and waterfalls. Here, too, are coffee plantations, cattle ranches, and even a royal palace. On the top of Mauna Kea Mountain, there is an observatory where scientists can get wonderful views of the night sky. The Big Island also contains places important to native Hawaiian history: petroglyphs (pictures carved in rocks) and sacred places.

5   The Big Island is a fascinating place. You can ski on Mauna Kea Mountain, play golf on an active volcano, and then go snorkeling or scuba diving — all in the same day.

6 The Big Island is "another" Hawaii. It's not the Hawaii of crowds of tourists or modern office buildings. But it is a Hawaii worth seeing.

VOCABULARY

mist	*n.*	thin fog; low clouds containing very small drops of water
skyscrapers	*n.*	very tall buildings
resident	*n.*	someone who lives in a place, not a visitor
arid	*adj.*	dry
valleys	*n.*	the land between two hills or mountains (often with a river going through it)
streams	*n.*	very small rivers
plantations	*n.*	large pieces of land used to grow crops (especially tea, coffee, cotton, etc.)
cattle	*n.*	large 4-legged farm animals, raised for their meat or milk (such as cows)
ranch	*n.*	a very large farm for raising cattle
palace	*n.*	a place where a king or queen lives
observatory	*n.*	a place for observing (watching) the stars and planets in the night sky
sacred	*adj.*	important for religious purposes
fascinating	*adj.*	very interesting

AFTER READING 6.3

1. **Another good title for this article is**

    ____ **a.** The Many Islands of Hawaii   ____ **c.** Golfing in Hawaii

    ____ **b.** The Best Places to Stay on the Big Island   ____ **d.** The Many Faces of the Big Island

2. **Look at the map of Hawaii. Write the number that shows the location of each place. Write the letter showing the picture of each place.**

    # _4a_ Hilo is the only major city on the eastern coast. However, don't imagine skyscrapers. The center of town is mostly two- or three-story buildings.

    # ____ The northeast coast is a place where streams, wind, and waves have created high cliffs and deep valleys.

    # ____ The southern tip of the island is mainly a desert. Here, you can find petroglyphs.

    # ____ The west coast is well-known for its coffee plantations. They produce a kind of coffee known as "Kona" coffee.

    # ____ In the center of the northern region is the Parker Ranch. Here, cowboys raise cattle.

    # ____ In the middle of the island are the two highest peaks: Mauna Kea and Mauna Loa.

3. **Write *T* if the sentence is true. Write *F* if the sentence is false and correct it.**

    ____ **a.** The weather on the Big Island is the same everywhere.

    ____ **b.** The Big Island is smaller than Taiwan.

    ____ **c.** Kings or queens once lived on the Big Island.

LOOKING AT LANGUAGE

1. **One way to guess the meaning of words is to learn some word parts that have meaning. For example, the ending *-less* means *without*. Find the words in paragraph 1 which have the ending *-less*: _____ and _____. What do you think these words mean?**

2. **Look at each group of words. Three out of the four words are associated. One word is different. Circle the word that is different.**

a. streams	rivers	desert	waterfalls
b. palace	petroglyph	building	skyscraper
c. tourist	resident	traveler	visitor

CHALLENGE

How is your knowledge of geography? If you can answer 7 or more of these questions, you know quite a bit!

1. What percent of the Earth is covered by water?

    ____ **a.** about 28%   ____ **b.** about 47%   ____ **c.** about 71%

2. Which ocean is the deepest?

    ____ **a.** the Pacific Ocean   ____ **b.** the Atlantic Ocean   ____ **c.** the Indian Ocean

3. What percentage of Greenland is ice-free (that is, without permanent ice)?

    ____ **a.** 16%   ____ **b.** 48%   ____ **c.** 72%

4. Which country is landlocked (that is, surrounded on all sides by land)?

    ____ **a.** Poland   ____ **b.** Pakistan   ____ **c.** Bolivia

5. How many islands does Greece have?

    ____ **a.** fewer than 100   ____ **b.** between 100 and 1,000   ____ **c.** more than 2,000

6. Most of Greece is

    ____ **a.** flat   ____ **b.** mountainous   ____ **c.** desert-like

7. Which country has no active volcanoes?

    ____ **a.** Indonesia   ____ **b.** Italy   ____ **c.** Egypt

8. Which country does <u>not</u> touch the equator?

    ____ **a.** Colombia   ____ **b.** The Philippines   ____ **c.** Kenya

9. The Ganges is _____ to Hindu people in India.

    ____ **a.** a sacred river   ____ **b.** a sacred valley   ____ **c.** a sacred mountain

10. Which country contains no desert?

    ____ **a.** Chile   ____ **b.** Australia   ____ **c.** Turkey

QUOTES AND SAYINGS USING "LAND" WORDS	• *The grass is always greener on the other side.* • *Don't make a mountain out of a molehill.*

Below are two house plans. Look carefully at them. Notice where the bedrooms and bathrooms are. Notice if there is a patio. Imagine walking through the front door. What will you see first? Is this pleasing or not? Is this a practical house plan or not?

**Work in pairs to decide which plan you like best.
(Both houses are the same size.)**

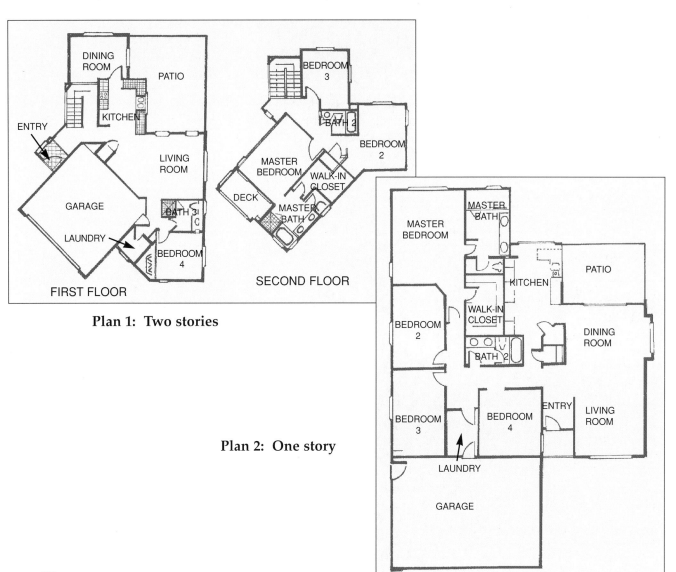

Plan 1: Two stories

Plan 2: One story

Draw a house plan showing your house or apartment. Show your drawing to a classmate and give him or her a "tour" of the house. (For example, "You enter through this door. There is a closet on the right. The room on your left is the kitchen. It has blue and white wallpaper. In the room, there is a stove, refrigerator...")

READING 7.1

The Herald

Friday, December 20

Survey: What do you like best about your home? What do you like least?

Miho Takeda
Architect

"I love my home because I designed it myself. I planned everything to fit my needs. For example, I love to cook so the kitchen is spacious and light. I have a lot of counter space. I guess that's my favorite room. What do I like least? The bills! I wanted a lot of windows in the house because I love light and fresh air but this causes my heating bills to go up. Oh, well. You can't have it all, can you?"

Phil Hunt
Mechanic

"I just moved into my own apartment last month and the thing I like best about it is that it's mine!!! If I don't want to clean, I don't have to. If I want to paint the walls green, I can. No one tells me what to do. The only thing I don't like are the cockroaches. I guess if I clean more often..."

Marcos Arias
Salesman

"My house is a pretty typical suburban home. Three bedrooms, two stories, a small backyard. I guess I like the fact that each of my daughters has her own bedroom. The house is big enough for my family to live in comfortably. What I don't like is that all the houses in the neighborhood look the same."

Heather Breceda
Student

"I don't like my house at all. It's in a really boring neighborhood. There are lots of kids in the neighborhood but none are my age. Well, there is one girl but we don't have anything in common. And my house...it's too small for our family. I have to share my room with my two sisters. If I could, I would move into my own apartment in the city. I wouldn't care what it looked like."

Paulo Tonelli
Retired

"I built my house 50 years ago with my own hands when my wife and I first got married. This house is full of so many memories. Each room contains things that remind me of people and events from the past. There is the piano that my wife played. There is the rocking chair that my children loved. That's the best thing about this house — the memories it holds for me... and now with my wife and kids gone, those memories are so important. The worst thing? Well, the house is getting old just like me. We both don't work as well as we used to. It needs a lot of repairs."

Ok Hee Moon
Housewife

"I can see the mountains from my living room window and that's what I love best about my apartment. I grew up in a part of Korea that was very mountainous, so this view reminds me of my childhood. What I like least is the design. I would like more closets and a bigger living room".

YOUR TURN

What do you like best about your house? What do you like least?

44

UNDERSTANDING

1. **Look at these rooms and houses. Read the survey on page 44 and decide who probably lives in these places. Write their names under the picture.**

_____ _____ _____

_____ _____

2. **Check (√) the correct box or boxes.**

	Miho	Phil	Marcos	Heather	Paulo	Ok Hee
a. Who doesn't like his or her neighborhood?						
b. Who wants more room?						
c. Who lives with his or her family?						

3. Paulo remembers his _____ when he sees the piano and Ok Hee remembers her _____ when she looks out her living room window.

4. **Put a + in front of the sentence if it is a good thing about a house. Put a − in front of the sentence if it is a bad thing.**

___ **a.** Everything fits my needs.

___ **b.** The kitchen is spacious.

___ **c.** The heating bills are high.

___ **d.** I have cockroaches.

___ **e.** It's big enough for my family to live in comfortably.

___ **f.** It's in a boring neighborhood.

___ **g.** It's too small.

VOCABULARY PRACTICE: HOME REPAIRS

Read about the house problem and decide who you need to call. Fill in the blank with one of these words, using each word only once:

plumber	electrician	carpenter	painter
appliance repairperson	gardener	locksmith	roofer

1. The paint on the wall is chipping. Call a _____.
2. Why aren't the lights working? We need to call the _____.
3. The refrigerator isn't working. Can you call the _____?
4. Uh-oh. All my grass is dying. Call the _____.
5. This faucet keeps dripping. We need to call a _____.
6. I'm having a hard time opening the door. The key isn't working. Let's call a _____.
7. I'd like to build another room onto the house. Do you know a good _____?

READING 7.2

Many businesses provide services to homeowners. Look at this page of ads from a local newspaper.

Classified Ads

SERVICES

APPLIANCE REPAIR

We're there in minutes to do the job right, at the best possible price. Any major kitchen or laundry appliance repaired.

Call Pat 723-4289.

BRICK/ MASONRY

MGO
Construction.

Masonry, concrete, tile. Patios. Driveways.
Licensed. 559-2943

CARPENTRY

New cabinets, doors, windows, staircases, room additions, 10 years' experience.

Call Jay 661-2300.

Cleaning

Vic's Cleaning Services
Residential/Business.
Reasonable rates.
Call **Vic**: 223-0698.

MARY'S MAIDS
Housecleaning
Reliable, energetic, honest women. Experienced.

Weekly/biweekly.
Can provide references.
Call 896-4089
and leave message.

ELECTRICAL

ABC Electric

We take care of everything electrical: ceiling fans, lights.
Prompt.
Fast.
Reasonable.
Licensed.

John, 943-3980.

HANDYMAN

I CAN FIX IT ALL.
Home repairs, painting, fences, tile, brick.
Phil. 724-2349.

LANDSCAPING

Ken's *Gardening*

Planting, clean-ups, maintenance, tree trimming.

In business since 1988.

378-1480

PAINTING

Sun Painting
Interiors, Exteriors.
Home, apartments.
Free estimates. 25 years of experience.
Call Kim at
816-8809, 9:00-5:00.

Plumbing

All types of plumbing and drain service. 24-hour service. Phone estimates.

Ray or Lenny
575-4980

ROOFING

TIP TOP
Roofing

Re-roof or repair. We'll do it.
Call Jan, 875-9087 or fax 875-9080.

FOR SALE

VOCABULARY

masonry	*n.*	work done with stone or brick
estimate	*n.*	a statement of how much something will probably cost
residential	*adj.*	relating to a home
rates	*n.*	charges; fees
reliable	*adj.*	dependable; trustworthy
energetic	*adj.*	full of energy
prompt	*adj.*	on time; not late

licensed	*adj.*	having an official paper showing that one can do something
landscaping	*n.*	making land more beautiful by adding plants
maintenance	*n.*	keeping something in good condition
references	*n.*	letters about someone's work or character (used when looking for a job)

SCANNING

How many can you answer in 2 minutes? Write *T* if the sentence is true; write *F* if the sentence is false and correct it.

____ 1. Tip Top Roofing only builds new roofs.

____ 2. The number for Mary's Maids Cleaning Service is 896-4089.

____ 3. Jay, the carpenter, has a year of experience doing carpentry.

____ 4. Pat's Appliance Repair fixes appliances and TVs.

____ 5. Ken's Gardening Company is only 5 years old.

____ 6. John, the electrician, is licensed.

____ 7. Mary's Maids, the housecleaners, can give references.

____ 8. Ray, the plumber, is open all day and night.

____ 9. Vic, the cleaner, only cleans businesses.

____ 10. You can call Jan, the roofer, at 875-9078.

____ 11. Pat, the appliance repairperson, can fix a refrigerator.

____ 12. Pat, the appliance repairperson, will come to your house.

____ 13. ABC Electric only repairs lights.

____ 14. If you need to know how much something will probably cost, Ray, the plumber can tell you over the phone.

____ 15. Phil, the handyman, can do painting and masonry.

LOOKING AT LANGUAGE

1. The word parts *ex-* and *in-* mean *out* and *in*. Sun Painting does interior and exterior work. What does that mean? _____

2. The word part *re-* means *again*. Tip Top roofing does re-roofing and repairs. What does *re-roofing* mean? _____

3. Mary's Maids, the housecleaners, work weekly or biweekly. The word part *bi-* means *two*. What does *biweekly* mean? _____

4. Look at the Mary's Maids housecleaning ad. What adjectives do they use to describe themselves? _____, _____, _____, and _____

5. Look at the ABC Electric ad. Which adjective does John use to describe his prices?

_____

BEFORE READING 7.3

Look at the title and the picture. What do you think this article will be about?
Check (√) your answer.

_____ lowering the prices of buildings
_____ building underground
_____ building taller skyscrapers
_____ making buildings safe during earthquakes

Skim the reading to see if your guess is correct. To skim, read the first paragraph, the
first line of each paragraph in the middle, and the last paragraph.

READING 7.3

Building Down Not Up

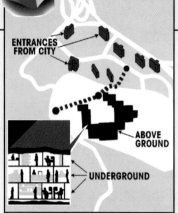

ENTRANCES FROM CITY

ABOVE GROUND

UNDERGROUND

1   In 1901, H.G. Wells, an American science fiction writer, wrote a book describing
a trip to the moon. When the explorers landed on the moon, they discovered that
the moon was full of countless underground cities. They expressed their surprise
to the "moon people" they met. In turn, the "moon people" expressed *their*
surprise. "Why," they asked, "are you traveling to *outer* space when you don't
even use your *inner* space?"

2   In 1901, H.G. Wells could only imagine travel to the moon. In 1969, human
beings really did land on the moon. People today know that there are no
underground cities on the moon. However, the question that the "moon people"
asked is still an interesting one. A growing number of people — engineers,
geologists, architects — are seriously thinking about it.

3   Underground systems are already in place. Many cities have underground parking garages. In some cities, such
as Tokyo, Seoul and Montreal, there are large underground shopping areas. The "Chunnel", a tunnel connecting
England and France, is now complete. Subway systems are common in many cities.

4   But what about underground cities? Japan's Taisei Corporation is designing a network of underground systems,
called "Alice Cities." (Alice is a character in a well-known children's story, *Alice in Wonderland*, who falls down a
rabbit hole and finds another world.) The designers imagine using surface space for public parks and using underground
space for apartments, offices, garages, shopping, and so on. A solar dome would cover the whole city.

5   Supporters of underground development say that building down rather than building up is a good way to use
the earth's space. The surface, they say, can be used for farms, parks, gardens, and wilderness. H.G. Wells' "moon
people" would agree. Would you?

VOCABULARY

science fiction	*n.*	books and stories about an imagined future
explorers	*n.*	people who travel to a new place to discover new things
engineers	*n.*	people who plan machines, roads, bridges, and so on
geologists	*n.*	people who study the earth's geology (such as its rocks, land)
architects	*n.*	people who design buildings and houses
systems	*n.*	a group of parts working together
tunnel	*n.*	an underground road
network	*n.*	a group of systems which cross or meet one another
surface	*n.*	the outer part
solar	*adj.*	using the energy of the sun
dome	*n.*	a round roof on a building
supporters	*n.*	people who believe in something or agree with something
to develop	*v.*	to make bigger or more complete or more widely used
wilderness	*n.*	land in its natural form (not developed by humans)

UNDERSTANDING

1. Another title for this article could be
   ___ a. The History of Underground Development
   ___ b. Underground Development: Real and Imagined
   ___ c. The Good and Bad Side of Underground Development
   ___ d. The Moon's Underground Cities

2. Which picture best shows H.G. Wells' story? Check (√) the picture.

3. Which paragraph gives examples of present underground systems? Paragraph #____.

4. Which paragraph tells about a possible design for the future? Paragraph #____.

5. Write *T* if the sentence is true. Write *F* if the sentence is false and correct it.

   ___ a. H.G. Wells traveled to the moon.
   ___ b. People already use underground systems.
   ___ c. The plans for the "Alice Cities" contain underground parks.

LOOKING AT LANGUAGE

1. Look at the first line:

In 1901, H.G. Wells, an American science fiction writer, wrote a book describing a trip to the moon.

The phrase "an American science fiction writer" is added to the main sentence so the reader knows who H.G. Wells is. Underline the added phrase in the following sentences:
   a. May Ndubuisi, a restaurant owner and Nigerian cook, says "It's the richest soup we make."
   b. George Parma, Martina Navratilova's first professional coach, lived and worked in Prague.
   c. The Chunnel, a tunnel connecting England and France, is now complete.

2. Look at the word that is circled. What is its reference? Draw an arrow to the word or words.
   a. The question that the "moon people" asked is still an interesting one. A growing number of people are seriously thinking about it.
   b. Supporters of underground development say that building down rather than building up is a good way to use the earth's space. The surface, they say, can be used for farms.

THINK ABOUT IT

What do you think of underground development? Would you ever live in an underground city?

CHALLENGE

All of the words in the crossword puzzle are in Unit 7. Can you complete the puzzle?

Across Clues
1. a statement of how much something will probably cost
7. the area around a house (including other houses and stores, for example)
8. a place where someone grows food and sometimes raises animals
11. a word part meaning "again"
12. fix
13. a place to keep your car
15. a place to keep your clothes

Down Clues
1. a word part meaning "out"
2. an underground road
3. a man who can do a lot of different repairs around the house
4. a natural place (not developed by humans)
5. on time
6. a _____ chair moves back and forth
9. a person who designs houses and buildings
10. a person who fixes pipes and drains
14. price; charge; fee

QUOTES AND SAYINGS ABOUT HOMES

• *East, west, home's best.*

• *It is easier to tear a house down than build it up.*

Work in groups of three. Your job, as a group, is to plan a small party (up to 10 people, including yourselves) for next week. However, this is not a typical party. You can invite anyone in the world...and they will come. (They must be living, though!)

Work with your group to decide the following:
- who are you going to invite?
- when are you going to have the party?
- where are you going to have the party?
- what are you going to serve?
- what are you going to do at the party?

When you finish planning, tell the rest of the class about the party you planned. After you hear about all the parties, decide which party you think will be the most fun or the most interesting.

READING 8.1

Carlos lives in Brazil. Read the letters he and Roni wrote each other.

SOFTECH

Dear Roni,

How are you? We aren't very good at staying in touch by mail, are we? Oh well, seeing each other in person is better!

That's why I'm writing. I need to go to Los Angeles on business from July 1st to 14th and I know you're not too far from L.A. What are your plans for those two weeks? Would it be possible to spend some time together?

All the best,
Carlos

SOFTECH

Dear Roni,

This is getting complicated...but I think we can work something out. I won't have a car so I would appreciate your driving up here. I hope you don't mind.

I think the 12th will work the best. I have business meetings all day on the 11th and 13th. I have a breakfast meeting on the 12th, but it's early so it won't interfere with our day.

Why don't you plan to be here around 11 a.m? I'll be staying at the Plaza Hotel. We can go out for an early lunch and then spend the rest of the day together. I'm looking forward to seeing you.

Until then,
Carlos

P.S. Rosa and the kids won't be joining me this time. They send their love.

Hello Carlos,

Great news!! I'd love to see you in July. Will you be coming with Rosa and the kids or by yourself?

July is a pretty busy month for me but I think if we plan now, we can find time. I will be out of town from July 1st to the 10th. It's my mom's 65th birthday and the family is planning a surprise party for her on the fifth in New York. I also volunteer at the library once a week. I'm scheduled for the 14th and I'd rather not change that. It looks like the 11th, 12th or 13th would work best for me. Would you like me to drive up to L.A. and visit with you there or would you like to drive down here? It takes about 1½ hours.

Let me know as soon as possible about your plans and we'll decide on something definite.

Best wishes,
Roni

RSL

Dear Carlos,

It's on my calendar. July 12th, 11 a.m. I'll meet you in the hotel lobby. See you then!! Love to Rosa and the kids.

Warm regards,
Roni

VOCABULARY

to stay in touch	v.	to communicate by phone or by letter or in person
to volunteer	v.	to offer your time without pay
definite	adj.	certain; sure
complicated	adj.	difficult to understand or arrange
to work something out	v.	to find an answer to a problem
I hope you don't mind.	=	I hope it is not a problem for you.
to interfere	v.	to get in the way of doing something
lobby	n.	a large entrance hallway, often used as a waiting area (in a hotel or hospital, for example)

UNDERSTANDING

1. **Fill in the important dates on Roni's calendar and Carlos' calendar below. Write where they will be and what they will be doing.**

Roni's Calendar   Carlos' Calendar

JULY   **JULY**

1	_____
2	_____
3	_____
4	_____
5	_____
6	_____
7	_____
8	_____
9	_____
10	_____
11	_____
12	_____
13	_____
14	_____

J U L Y

1	_____
2	_____
3	_____
4	_____
5	_____
6	_____
7	_____
8	_____
9	_____
10	_____
11	_____
12	_____
13	_____
14	_____

J U L Y

2. **Write *T* if the sentence is true. Write *F* if the sentence is false and correct it. Write *?* if you don't know from the letters.**

_____ **a.** Roni and Carlos write each other often.
_____ **b.** Roni lives in Los Angeles.
_____ **c.** Carlos doesn't like to drive.
_____ **d.** Roni knows how to drive.
_____ **e.** Roni is going to travel during the month of July.
_____ **f.** Rosa and the kids are going to be in L.A. with Carlos.
_____ **g.** Roni will meet Carlos on July 12th outside the hotel.

VOCABULARY PRACTICE: PARTIES

People have parties for many different reasons. Match the party with the reason.

_____ a wedding party   **a.** Joe and Bea got married on this date 15 years ago.
_____ an anniversary party   **b.** Tim and Rosa just moved into a new home.
_____ a housewarming party   **c.** Cass was born on this day 1 year ago.
_____ a birthday party   **d.** Maria is going to have a baby next month.
_____ a graduation party   **e.** Carolina just finished college.
_____ a baby shower   **f.** Linda and Jose got married today.

Which of these kinds of parties do you have?

What other kinds of parties do your friends and family have?

53

READING 8.2

Read the invitations to these parties.

1.

> Raul and Lidia Solis
> Robert and Ellen Gates
> would be honored
> to have you share in the joy
> of the marriage of their children
>
> *Norma*
>
> and
>
> *Ralph*
>
> The wedding ceremony will be held on
> Sunday, the ninth of September
> at five o'clock
> at The Bay Club, Coral Beach.
> A reception will follow the ceremony
>
> R.S.V.P. by August 10

2.

You're invited!

> Dear Ron and Gary,
>   Are you free on Saturday, the 3rd of August?
> A few friends are visiting from out of town and
> we'd like to have a small dinner party for them.
>   It would be great if you can join us.
>   Love,
>   Alex and Carol

3.

Shhhh! Don't say a word!

IT'S A SURPRISE!

Please help celebrate a special person's birthday

Who:	*Freddy's 30th Birthday!*
When:	*Aug. 4th, 6:30 pm*
Where:	*Lynn's house, 12 Pine St.*

Please R.S.V.P. to: *Lynn, 873-3032*

VOCABULARY

to be honored	*v.*	to feel proud because of respect received from others
joy	*n.*	happiness
reception	*n.*	a formal party
R.S.V.P.	=	(French: Répondez s'il vous plaît) These letters mean that the senders of the invitation want you to tell them if you can or can't come

SCANNING

How many questions can you answer about the three invitations on page 54 in 2 minutes?

1. Which invitation is to a surprise party?   Invitation # _____
2. Which invitation is to a wedding?   Invitation # _____
3. What is the date of the wedding ceremony?   _____
4. What is the time of the wedding ceremony?   _____
5. Whose birthday is it in invitation #3?   _____
6. Who is giving a party in invitation #2?   _____ and _____
7. What is the date of the party in invitation #2?   _____
8. What is the name of the bride (the woman who is getting married)?   _____
9. What is the name of the groom (the man who is getting married)?   _____
10. What time is the surprise party?   _____

UNDERSTANDING

1. Match the invitations to the pictures. Write *1*, *2*, or *3* next to the correct picture.

Invitation # _____

Invitation # _____

Invitation # _____

2. Look at invitation #1. Who are Raul and Linda Solis? _____ .
    Who are Robert and Ellen Gates? _____ .

3. Invitations #1 and #3 say R.S.V.P. at the end. What should the receiver of the
    invitation do? _____ .

TALK ABOUT IT

1. Do people have surprise birthday parties in your family? Do people bring
    gifts to birthday parties? If so, do people open the gifts at the party or after
    the party?

2. Do you and your family have dinner parties at home with friends or do
    you more often go to restaurants with them? What is a good gift to bring
    to hosts of a dinner party, in your opinion?

BEFORE READING 8.3

In many newspapers, there are advice columns. These columns have names such as "Dear Abby" or "Dear Ann Landers" or "Ask Susie." People write letters and hope to receive good advice. Do newspapers written in your language have advice columns? Do you read them?

Below is an advice column called "Ask Sally." First read the letters. Talk with your classmates about possible advice you could give the letter writer. Then, read what "Sally" advises. You may or may not agree with her.

READING 8.3

Ask Sally

DEAR SALLY: I recently became engaged. I love my fiancé a lot but we are getting into a lot of arguments about our wedding plans. I would prefer a small wedding, just our immediate family and closest friends. I think it is such a special moment and I only want the people who are most important to be near us. I don't want to be surrounded by people who don't really care about us. He wants the whole world to be there — the mail carrier, the baker, the butcher!!! My fiancé says a wedding day is the most important day in anyone's life. He wants to share his joy with everyone.

It's not a question of money although I do worry about how much a wedding costs and I would rather save the money for a house. I hate fighting but I just don't feel comfortable with his plans.

---NERVOUS

DEAR NERVOUS: Planning weddings can be very stressful. Each person has clear ideas about what his or her "perfect" wedding should be. Each person has dreams and hopes for that day.

Now is a good time to practice compromising with your husband-to-be. Neither one of you should be unhappy on your wedding day. If you get your way, your husband will be unhappy. If he gets his way, it sounds as if you will be unhappy.

Why don't the two of you talk about a compromise? Perhaps a medium-sized wedding? Perhaps two weddings — a small intimate ceremony and a large reception? You will have to compromise many times in your married life. You both can start now.

DEAR SALLY: Tomorrow is my wife's and my 10th anniversary. I want to surprise her with something special but we're broke. Do you have any ideas?

---IN LOVE BUT
OUT OF MONEY

DEAR IN LOVE: There are many ways to show your wife that you love her without spending a lot of money. Prepare a special meal. Write a poem for her. Take her to a romantic spot to look at the stars. Use your imagination. If it comes from your heart, she'll appreciate it.

VOCABULARY

to get engaged	*v.*	to make a promise to each other to get married
fiancé	*n.*	the man to whom a woman is engaged (a fiancée is the woman to whom a man is engaged)
arguments	*n.*	disagreements; fights
immediate family	*n.*	the closest members of the family (usually parents and siblings)
stressful	*adj.*	causing anxiety, tension, worry
to compromise	*v.*	to come to an agreement that is a middle position between the two sides
intimate	*adj.*	very close and personal
to be broke	*v.*	(informal) to be out of money

AFTER READING 8.3

1. In the first letter, NERVOUS gives her viewpoint about the wedding and her reasons. Then, she gives her fiancé's viewpoint and his reasons. Fill in the blanks with the correct information.

   NERVOUS' viewpoint about the wedding: she wants _____ .
   The fiancé's viewpoint about the wedding: he wants _____ .

2. Why does NERVOUS feel the way she does? (Check two)
   ____ a. She only wants to share this special moment with people she loves and people who love her.
   ____ b. She only wants to share this special moment with her fiancé.
   ____ c. She doesn't like the mail carrier, the baker, or the butcher.
   ____ d. She would rather save the money instead of spending it on the wedding.

3. Why does the fiancé feel the way he does?
   ____ a. He wants to share this special moment with everyone.
   ____ b. He only wants to share this special moment with people he loves and people who love him.
   ____ c. He only wants to share this special moment with his fiancée.
   ____ d. He doesn't like the mail carrier, the baker, or the butcher.

4. What is Sally's main advice to NERVOUS?
   ____ a. Do it your husband's way.   ____ c. Think of a new idea together.
   ____ b. Do it your way.   ____ d. Ask your parents for advice.

5. Sally answers IN LOVE and says, "There are many ways to show your wife that you love her without spending money." How many ways does she suggest?

   ____ a. 1   ____ b. 2   ____ c. 3   ____ d. 4

LOOKING AT LANGUAGE

1. Sally says "*Neither* one of you should be unhappy on your wedding day." Sally could also say "Neither you nor your fiancé should be unhappy on your wedding day." Both sentences mean you shouldn't be unhappy and your fiancé shouldn't be unhappy. Consider the following sentences:

   a. Neither the husband nor the wife has money.
      Who has money?   ____ the husband   ____ the wife   ____ no one

   b. Neither the butcher nor the baker can come to the wedding.
      Who can come to the wedding?   ____ the butcher   ____ the baker
                                          ____ not the butcher and not the baker

2. The word *unhappy* means *not happy*. The prefix *un-* means *not*. Check the words below where *un-* means *not*.
   ____ unsafe   ____ under   ____ unkind   ____ unafraid   ____ unusual

THINK ABOUT IT

1. Do you agree with Sally's advice to NERVOUS? If not, what are your ideas?
2. Do you have other suggestions for IN LOVE BUT OUT OF MONEY?

CHALLENGE

Lidia, Paul, Suha, Rita and David all have plans for tomorrow evening. After reading the clues, can you figure out where each person is going and what time each party starts? They are all going to different parties and each party starts at a different time: 7:00, 7:30, 8:00, 8:30 or 9:00. (Hint: Paul and David are men. Lidia, Suha, and Rita are women.)

1. The woman who is going to the graduation party is Rita's best friend.

2. The graduation party begins 2 hours earlier than the wedding party.

3. Paul's party starts the latest of all.

4. Neither men are going to the housewarming party.

5. Lidia is going to a dinner party.

6. The housewarming party begins earlier than the birthday party.

7. David's party begins at 8:00.

If you think you know the answers, fill in the blanks below.

_____ is going to the _____ party which begins at 7:00.

_____ is going to the _____ party which begins at 7:30.

_____ is going to the _____ party which begins at 8:00.

_____ is going to the _____ party which begins at 8:30.

_____ is going to the _____ party which begins at 9:00.

GIFT GIVING AROUND THE WORLD:

WHAT NOT TO GIVE!!!

- In some parts of Latin America, avoid giving thirteen of anything (an unlucky number) or handkerchiefs (associated with crying).

- In some parts of China, avoid giving clocks. (The sound of the word for "clock" in Chinese is associated with death.)

- In some parts of Japan, avoid giving gifts in groups of four. (The sound of the word for "four" in Japanese is associated with death.)

- In some parts of France, avoid giving chrysanthemum flowers. (These flowers are associated with death.)

The game below is called "Find someone who..." To play, you need to talk to your classmates and ask them questions. When you find someone who fits a description, write his or her name on the line. For example, #1 says, "find someone who is in a good mood today." You must ask someone *"Are you in a good mood today?"* If your classmate says *No*, ask the same question to someone else. If your classmate says *Yes*, write his or her name on the line next to the question. After 10 minutes, your teacher will ask you to stop talking. The person with the most names wins!

1. Find someone who is in a good mood today. _____

2. Find someone who is in a bad mood today. _____

3. Find someone who feels nervous right now. _____

4. Find someone who feels angry right now. _____

5. Find someone who is sad right now. _____

6. Find someone who is hungry right now. _____

7. Find someone who is worried right now. _____

8. Find someone who is excited about something today. _____

9. Find someone who is tired right now. _____

10. Find someone who is energetic right now. _____

When the game is over, talk to your classmates and ask for details about their answers. For example, if someone said she feels angry, you can ask *"Why do you feel angry?"*

59

READING 9.1

The Herald

Sunday, November 2

Survey: What puts you in a bad mood?
How do you get out of your bad moods?

Marie Rene School counselor	**Laura Bravo** Student	**Cuong Nguyen** Retired	**Luis Velez** Student	**John Winn** Businessman	**Lee Ming Lam** Engineer

"I get into a bad mood when I have to drive in traffic. I just feel so frustrated because there's nothing I can do about it. I try a lot of techniques to stay calm — listening to relaxing music, for example — but nothing works."

"I get in a bad mood when I have to do schoolwork or housework. I know I have responsibilities and I try to take care of them but sometimes I just want to be carefree. I get out of these bad moods by promising myself something special when I finish my work so I might say to myself, "Laura, when you finish your homework, you can go out for some ice cream.""

"I rarely get into bad moods. I'm pretty content with life. I have a wonderful wife and children, a nice home, and my health. Every morning, I take a long walk around a lake near my house. This calms me. If I ever feel sad, I think about the good things I have and I immediately feel better."

"I get into a bad mood when I work really hard on something but don't get the grade or the reaction I want. For example, I wrote a paper for my history class. I probably spent 20 hours on it. I thought it was an "A" paper but I only got a "B." Or another time, I tried to get my girlfriend a really special gift for her birthday. I went to about 50 stores and finally found a necklace I liked. I was really happy about it but when I gave it to her, she smiled but she didn't seem really excited. That made me feel disappointed. What do I do to get out of my bad mood? I just tell myself, "That's life!""

"I get into a bad mood when my boss doesn't appreciate what I do. Yesterday, someone else in the office got a promotion but I think I'm better than he is. That really put me into a bad mood. But what can you do? Sometimes, life isn't fair. One way I get out of a bad mood is by doing exercises. I go to a gym and lift weights. I think exercise helps."

"I get into a bad mood when I read the newspaper or watch the news on TV and see all the terrible things in the world — war, hunger, poverty. Why can't we learn to live together and share the earth's riches? I guess I'm a dreamer. How do I get out of my bad moods? I go to a park or the beach and look at nature. A beautiful sunset reminds me how special the earth is."

YOUR TURN

What puts you in a bad mood? How do you get out of your bad moods?

UNDERSTANDING

1. Check (√) the correct box or boxes.

	Marie	Laura	Cuong	Luis	John	Lee Ming
a. Who feels good when they spend time in nature?						
b. Who can't get out of her bad moods?						
c. Who is usually happy with life?						

2. Look at the survey on page 60. Draw a line to match the drawings to the names.

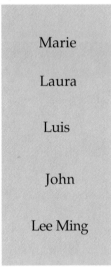

Marie

Laura

Luis

John

Lee Ming

VOCABULARY PRACTICE: MOODS AND FEELINGS

1. Look at the words in the box. All of them show moods or feelings. Put the words into two groups: positive or negative.

Positive Feelings

_____

_____

_____

_____

_____

Negative Feelings

_____

_____

_____

_____

_____

nervous	relaxed
happy	pleased
depressed	worried
content	calm
frustrated	disappointed
irritable	joyful

2. A good way to learn vocabulary is to use them in sentences that mean something to you. Try finishing these sentences about yourself.

a. I feel frustrated when _____.

b. I feel disappointed when _____.

c. I feel content when _____.

READING 9.2

Bobby McFerrin, an American jazz and pop singer, wrote the song "Don't Worry, Be Happy." This song became popular worldwide. (You may even see a few T-shirts which say "Don't Worry, Be Happy.") Here are the words to the song.

DON'T WORRY, BE HAPPY

Here's a little song I wrote.
You might want to sing it note for note,
   Don't worry, be happy.
In every life, we have some trouble.
When you worry, you make it double.
   Don't worry, be happy.
   Don't worry, be happy now.

      Don't worry,
      Be happy.
      Don't worry, be happy.

      Don't worry,
      Be happy.
      Don't worry, be happy.

Ain't got no place to lay your head.
Somebody came and took your bed.
   Don't worry, be happy.
Your landlord say your rent is late.
He may have to litigate.
   But don't worry. (Ha, ha, ha, ha, ha.)
   Be happy. (Look at me, I'm happy.)

SIMPLE PLEASURES

      Don't worry,
      Be happy.
      (Hey, I'll give you my phone number.
      When you worry, call me.
      I'll make you happy.)

      Don't worry.
      Be happy.

Ain't got no cash, ain't got no style.
Ain't got no gal to make you smile.
   But don't worry, be happy.
Cause when you worry, your face will frown
and that will bring everybody down.
   So don't worry, be happy.
   Don't worry, be happy now.

      Don't worry,
      Be happy.
      Don't worry, be happy.

      Don't worry,
      Be happy.
      Don't worry, be happy.

Now there, this song I wrote.
I hope you learned it note for note (like good little children)
    Don't worry, be happy (Listen to what I say)
In your life, expect some trouble.
When you worry, you make it double.
    Don't worry, be happy.
    Be happy now.

        Don't worry,
        Be happy,
        Don't worry, be happy.

        Don't worry,
        Be happy,
        Don't worry, be happy.

        Don't worry,
        Don't worry.
        Don't do it.

        Be happy.
        Put a smile on your face
        Don't bring everybody down.

        Don't worry,
        It will soon pass whatever it is.
        Don't worry, be happy.
        I'm not worried.
        I'm happy.

VOCABULARY

double	*n.*	something that is twice another in size or amount
to litigate	*v.*	to take someone to a law court
Ain't got no...	=	(slang) I don't have any...
cash	*n.*	(informal) money
style	*n.*	a special way of acting or dressing that others admire
gal	*n.*	(informal) woman
to frown	*v.*	to bring the eyebrows together to show you're unhappy
to bring someone down	*v.*	to make someone feel bad

note

UNDERSTANDING

1. **Which sentences express the views of the song, "Don't Worry, Be Happy."**
   (Check as many as are correct.)
   ____ **a.** Life is always good.   ____ **c.** When you worry, you make your problems bigger.
   ____ **b.** Bad things don't stay forever. ____ **d.** If you frown, other people will feel bad.

2. **What are some bad things that Bobby McFerrin names in his song?**
   (Check as many as are correct.)
   ____ **a.** Someone has no place to sleep.   ____ **c.** Someone has no girlfriend.
   ____ **b.** Someone has no money.   ____ **d.** Someone doesn't have the right clothes.

THINK ABOUT IT

What do you think of Bobby McFerrin's advice in his song?

BEFORE READING 9.3

The word *blue* means *sad*. Someone can say *I feel blue*. The word can also be a noun as in *she has the blues* (i.e., she feels depressed). Look at the title. "The Winter Blues." Look at the picture. Why might someone get the blues during the winter? Work as a class to think of reasons.

READING 9.3

THE WINTER BLUES

¹ It's November. The days are getting shorter. The nights are getting longer. And Mary, in London, is eating more, sleeping more, and feeling depressed. By February, the overeating, the oversleeping, and depression reach their peak. By April, Mary is back to normal. This pattern repeats itself year after year. Mary is not alone. There are others who suffer from the same symptoms all over the world — anywhere, in fact, where winter days are shorter and winter nights are longer.

² Researchers believe that Mary, and millions like her, suffer from a condition they call "Seasonal Affective Disorder," (SAD, for short). This condition is a kind of depression that comes with decreases in light exposure. The symptoms are fatigue, depression, irritability, increased appetite, and weight gain. Seasonal Affective Disorder, say the researchers, can affect anyone but most often affects women.

³ Fortunately, there are treatments for SAD. People with mild cases may improve just by brightening the rooms in their house and getting exposure to more sunlight. Many people with more severe cases can find relief with a new light treatment. With this treatment, SAD sufferers get between 30 minutes to a few hours a day of extra exposure to a special light (one that is five to twenty times brighter than typical indoor lighting). By increasing their exposure to either natural or artificial light, approximately 75% of people with SAD reduce their yearly symptoms.

⁴ Medical researchers tell people not to self-diagnose. SAD, they say, is a serious condition. A person with SAD has major depressions every winter, has improved moods in the spring and summer, and follows the same pattern each year. If you feel sad and irritable once in a while during the winter, you probably don't have SAD.

⁵ The new light treatment is changing the lives of people like Mary. Mary can now enjoy the seasonal changes, just as most of us do.

VOCABULARY

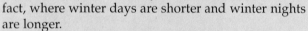

peak	*n.*	the highest point
pattern	*n.*	a design or event that repeats in the same way
to suffer	*v.*	to feel pain
symptoms	*n.*	signs of an illness
to decrease	*v.*	to become smaller in size or amount; to reduce
exposure	*n.*	the state of being open or unprotected in front of something
fatigue	*n.*	tiredness
appetite	*n.*	the feeling of wanting to eat food
to affect	*v.*	to cause some result in; to cause some change to
fortunately	*adv.*	luckily
treatment	*n.*	a way of taking care of an illness
to diagnose	*v.*	to name an illness or the cause of certain symptoms
major	*adj.*	serious; bigger and more important than others
once in a while	*adv.*	sometimes; now and then

AFTER READING 9.3

1. **The article talks about one cause of "the winter blues". What is the cause?**
   ____ **a.** the weather   ____ **c.** the increase in available light
   ____ **b.** the decrease in available light   ____ **d.** depression

   Before reading the article, you tried to think of reasons why someone might feel the "winter blues." Did you talk about the reason given in the article?

2. **Match the paragraph number with its main idea.**

Paragraph 2	**a.** Don't be quick to think you have SAD. Remember the differences between SAD and normal mood changes.
Paragraph 3	**b.** Many people with SAD can feel better if they receive exposure to extra light during winter months.
Paragraph 4	**c.** SAD is a kind of depression that has special symptoms and causes.

3. **Write _T_ if the sentence is true. Write _F_ if the statement is false and correct it.**

   _____ **a.** About 10,000 people in the world suffer from SAD.

   _____ **b.** Some SAD sufferers do not feel relief after increased exposure to light during winter months.

   _____ **c.** People with SAD usually lose weight during the winter months.

   _____ **d.** Both women and men can suffer from SAD.

   _____ **e.** Everyone who feels depressed in the winter is suffering from SAD.

LOOKING AT LANGUAGE

1. **You can guess the meaning of some of the vocabulary in the reading by looking for its opposite in the paragraph. Look at paragraph 3.**
   a. Which word in the paragraph is the opposite of "mild"? _____
   b. Which word in the paragraph is the opposite of "artificial"? _____

2. **The suffix _-er_ means _a person_. For example, the word _teacher_ is a _person who teaches_.**
   a. Find 2 words in the reading that have this suffix: _____ and _____ .
   b. Think of three other words that use this suffix: _____, _____, and _____ .

3. **Look at the word that is circled. What is its reference? Draw an arrow to the word or words.**
   a. It's November. And Mary, in London, is eating more, sleeping more, and feeling depressed. By February, the overeating, the oversleeping, and depression reach their peak. By April, Mary is back to normal. This pattern repeats itself year after year.
   b. Researchers believe that Mary, and millions like her, suffer from a condition they call "Seasonal Affective Disorder," (SAD, for short).

CHALLENGE

Can you find 20 words related to moods and feelings in this puzzle? You may find the words vertically (↕), horizontally (↔), or diagonally (↗) or (↘). A word list is given below the puzzle, but first try to find the words without the word list. It's more of a challenge!

L	I	P	L	E	A	S	E	D	E	A	N	E	R
H	A	R	A	F	O	N	E	R	V	O	U	S	A
E	A	D	I	R	R	I	T	A	B	L	E	R	N
N	D	P	I	U	A	H	O	F	E	H	N	E	D
P	J	E	P	S	J	A	C	R	I	A	B	R	E
R	O	P	P	T	A	P	H	A	P	P	E	P	T
O	Y	A	Y	R	Y	P	O	I	L	Y	N	O	N
O	F	A	C	A	E	Y	P	D	U	M	E	D	O
B	U	P	O	T	S	S	T	O	N	R	R	I	T
O	L	I	N	E	T	A	S	K	I	A	G	R	I
R	N	U	T	D	A	N	D	E	B	N	E	M	R
E	N	T	E	X	C	I	T	E	D	G	T	O	E
D	H	U	N	G	R	Y	W	O	R	R	I	E	D
L	O	O	T	N	E	R	V	I	N	Y	C	D	D

pleased, excited, worried, joyful, frustrated, afraid, energetic, blue, depressed, calm, irritable, hungry, bored, content, happy, angry, tired, sad, disappointed, nervous

QUOTES AND SAYINGS ABOUT MOODS AND FEELINGS

- "Happiness? That's nothing more than health and a poor memory." *Albert Schweitzer*
- "When I look back on all these worries, I remember the story of the old man who said on his deathbed that he had a lot of trouble in his life — most of which never happened!" *Winston Churchill*

There are many stories and poems about "homes." Here are a few. The first two are by Sandra Cisneros. Cisneros was born in Chicago in the United States in 1954. She is the daughter of a Mexican father and a Mexican-American mother. She writes poetry and short stories. These stories are from her book, <u>The House on Mango Street.</u> In these stories, the speaker is Esperanza, a young girl growing up in a poor area of Chicago. The third poem is by James Masao Mitsui. Mitsui was born in Washington State in the U.S. in 1940. Both his parents were Japanese immigrants. He is a high school teacher and author of three books of poetry.

Bums in the Attic
by Sandra Cisneros

1   I want a house on a hill like the ones with the gardens where Papa works. We go on Sundays, Papa's day off. I used to go. I don't anymore. You don't like to go out with us, Papa says. Getting too old? Getting too stuck-up, says Nenny.* I don't tell them I am ashamed — all of us staring out the window like the hungry. I am tired of looking at what we can't have. When we win the lottery...Mama begins, and then I stop listening.

2   People who live on hills sleep so close to the stars they forget those of us who live too much on earth. They don't look down at all except to be content to live on hills. They have nothing to do with last week's garbage or fear of rats. Night comes. Nothing wakes them but the wind.

3   One day, I'll own my own house, but I won't forget who I am or where I came from. Passing bums will ask, Can I come in? I'll offer them the attic, ask them to stay, because I know how it is to be without a house.

4   Some days after dinner, guests and I will sit in front of a fire. Floorboards will squeak upstairs. The attic grumble.

Rats? they'll ask.

Bums, I'll say, and I'll be happy.

*Esperanza's sister

VOCABULARY

stuck-up	*adj.*	describing someone who thinks they are better than others
ashamed	*adj.*	embarrassed
to stare	*v.*	to look for a long time without closing one's eyes
lottery	*n.*	a game where you buy a ticket with numbers on it and hope to win money
fear	*n.*	the feeling of being afraid or scared
to squeak	*v.*	to make a high but not loud sound
to grumble	*v.*	to make a low sound like thunder

TALK ABOUT IT

1. What does the Papa like to do every Sunday? Why?
2. Why doesn't Esperanza, the writer of the story, want to go anymore?
3. How does Esperanza imagine life on the hill?
4. What does Esperanza want in the future?
5. Why will she be happy to have bums staying in her attic?

A House of My Own
by Sandra Cisneros

Not a flat. Not an apartment in back. Not a man's house. Not a daddy's. A house all my own. With my porch and my pillow, my pretty purple petunias. My books and my stories. My two shoes waiting beside the bed. Nobody to shake a stick at. Nobody's garbage to pick up after.

Only a house quiet as snow, a space for myself to go, clean as paper before the poem.

porch

petunias

VOCABULARY

flat	*n.*	an apartment
to shake	*v.*	to move quickly up and down

TALK ABOUT IT

1. In this story, Esperanza imagines her own house. What does she want? What doesn't she want?

2. Cisneros writes that the house will be "quiet as snow" and "clean as paper before the poem." How do her words help you imagine this home?

Allowance
by James Masao Mitsui

I am ten.
My mother sits in a black
rocking chair in the parlor
and tells stories of a country school
surrounded by ricefields
and no roads.

I stand in the kerosene light
behind her,
earning my allowance.
A penny
for each white hair I pull.

VOCABULARY

allowance	*n.*	money a child gets each week from his or her parents
parlor	*n.*	a room (in old-style houses) for talking to guests or reading
kerosene light	*n.*	a light which burns oil (not using electricity)

TALK ABOUT IT

1. Mitsui does not give you a lot of information. He is just painting a picture with a few words. Close your eyes and imagine the scene he describes. Tell your classmates about the scene you imagine.

2. Is the house modern or old? Why do you think that?

3. Are the mother and son close? What makes you feel this?

Below, on the left, are pictures of 10 parents. Can you match them with their child or children on the right? See if you can find any similarities in appearances. Work in pairs.

Parent or Parents

Child or Children

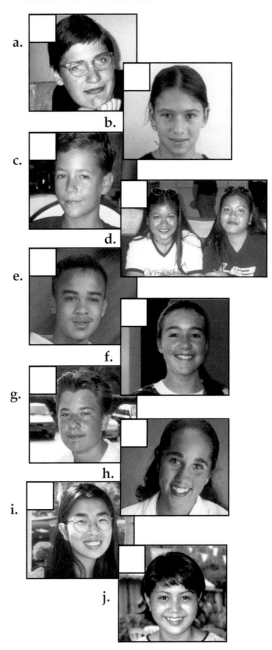

Talk to a classmate and ask these questions:

Do you look like either of your parents? If so, which one?

Who raised you — your parents, a relative, or someone else?

Were they strict or lenient?

Who chose your name — your mother? your father? a relative? someone else?

Why or how did they choose your name?

READING 11.1

R̲oni received this letter from her parents.

May 11th

Dear Roni,

You won't believe what kinds of things we found last weekend when we were cleaning out the garage! There were boxes and boxes of things that you and your brothers left there years and years ago. (We had to clear away a lot of dust and cobwebs to get to them!)

Two boxes were yours. When we opened them up, it brought back lots of memories. We found some drawings you did when you were 8 years old. You were a pretty good artist. We also found a stuffed animal -- a monkey. Do you remember that toy? You used to love it. We also found some of your books. You used to like to read a lot of mysteries. What else? Oh, yes. There was a small music box. It still works!!! And a little flute for children.

What would you like us to do with all of this? Please let us know.

Love,
Mom and Dad

Dear Mom and Dad,

I can't believe all of that stuff was in your garage!!! I'm sorry I wasn't there to help you clean up.

I do remember that monkey. I think Grandma and Grandpa gave it to me for one of my birthdays. I used to take it everywhere—even to bed. And that music box. I remember seeing it in a store window and falling in love with it. I saved money for months so I could buy it.

And the flute. It was the first musical instrument I ever played. I used to play the same three notes over and over and over . . . and over!!! But that led to bigger and better things. I can play more than 3 notes now on my saxophone and piano!!

What should you do with those things? Truthfully, I don't want them. I don't have enough room to store things. (On second thought, send the drawings. I'd like to see them.) Perhaps you can give the books to the local library or school. And as for the stuffed animal, the music box, and the flute, maybe Cassie would like something that was once her Aunt Roni's.

Love,
Roni

Here's Roni's answer.

VOCABULARY

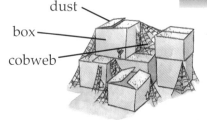

dust
box
cobweb

saxophone

flute

stuffed animals

stuff	*n.*	(informal) things, usually in a group (example: "I have a lot of stuff in my suitcase.")
to store	*v.*	to put something away for later use
on second thought	=	after thinking again (and usually changing one's mind)

UNDERSTANDING

1. **Where did Roni's parents find the boxes? Check (√) the box.**

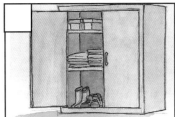  

2. **What did Roni's parents find in her boxes? Check (√) the correct boxes.**

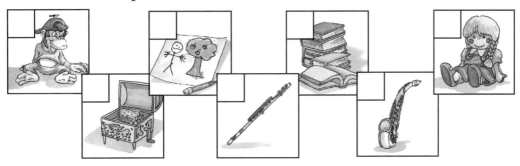

3. **How do you know no one looked in the boxes for a long time?**

_____

4. **Write *T* if the sentence is probably true. Write *F* if the sentence is probably false and correct it.**

_____ **a.** Roni doesn't want her parents to send anything.

_____ **b.** Cassie is Roni's niece.

_____ **c.** Roni had a live monkey when she was a child.

_____ **d.** Roni got the music box as a gift from her grandparents.

_____ **e.** Roni knows how to play the saxophone and piano.

TALK ABOUT IT

Do you still have objects from your childhood? What do you still have? Who saved those objects — you or your parents?

VOCABULARY PRACTICE: MUSICAL INSTRUMENTS

Answer the following questions about yourself.

1. Did you take music lessons when you were a child? If so, what instruments did you learn?

2. Did you have any toy musical instruments when you were a child? If so, what were they?

Fill in the blanks with the name of one or more musical instruments.

3. I love the sound of the _____.

4. I don't like the sound of the _____.

READING 11.2

The information below is from <u>The Baby Name Personality Survey</u> by Bruce Lansky and Barry Sinrod. In this book, the authors look at the meaning and origin of some common American/English girls' and boys' names. In addition, they look at the images that people have when they think of these names. (They got this information by surveying more than 75,000 parents.) Remember that the meaning and the origin of the names are facts; the images are people's feelings, only opinions.

	Name	Origin	Meaning	Image
GIRLS				
	Ann, Anne	Hebrew	graceful	"The name Ann calls to mind a plain, middle-class woman who is kind, practical."
	Amy	Latin	beloved	"People picture Amy as a small, slender woman who is quiet, calm, educated."
	Barbara	Latin	stranger	"The name Barbara has two different images: a heavy, plain, older woman who is nice and average or a small, pretty career woman who is very intelligent and a bit snobbish."
	Helen	Greek	light	"People picture Helen as a pretty, upper-class woman with dark hair and dark eyes who is graceful, smart, and well educated."
BOYS				
	David	Hebrew	beloved	"The name David calls to mind a strong, handsome, intelligent man who is friendly and dependable."
	George	Greek	farmer	"Most people think of George as an ordinary guy — a short, heavy, plain, older man who is quiet, kind, friendly and slow."
	Robert	Old English	bright fame	"The name Robert has two different images: a good-looking, strong athlete who is funny and outgoing or a stocky, average man who is quiet..."

VOCABULARY

origin	*n.*	where something comes from; the beginning
image	*n.*	a picture in one's mind
graceful	*adj.*	moving easily and beautifully
plain	*adj.*	simple; not pretty nor ugly
beloved	*adj.*	describing someone who receives love from others
slender	*adj.*	gracefully thin (in a positive way)
snobbish	*adj.*	describing someone who thinks he or she is better than others
dependable	*adj.*	reliable; describing someone you know will be there when needed
ordinary	*adj.*	average; typical
guy	*n.*	(informal) man
fame	*n.*	state of being famous, known
outgoing	*adj.*	describing someone who enjoys talking and being with groups of people
stocky	*adj.*	short, strong, and somewhat heavy (but not fat) in body

SCANNING

How many can you answer in 2 minutes?

1. Where does the name "George" come from? _____
2. What does the name "Helen" mean? _____
3. Which name means "stranger"? _____
4. Which name comes from Old English? _____
5. Which girl's name means "beloved"? _____
6. Which boy's name means "beloved"? _____
7. Where does the name "Barbara" come from? _____
8. Which name means "farmer"? _____
9. Which boy's name comes from Greek? _____
10. Which name means "graceful"? _____

UNDERSTANDING

1. Look at these two drawings. Which man would people probably imagine if they heard the name "David"? Which man would they imagine if they heard the name "George"? Write the name in the blank.

_____   _____

2. Answer *Yes* or *No*.

   a. Amy Johnson is a tall, heavy, outgoing woman. Does this match the image of her name? _____
   b. David Taylor is always willing to help his friends. Does this match the image of his name? _____
   c. George Hill is a good-looking athlete. Does this match the image of his name? _____
   d. Ann South is a rich and beautiful artist. Does this match the image of her name? _____
   e. Helen is a pretty blonde woman. Does this match the image of her name? _____
   f. Robert doesn't say too much. Does this match the image of his name? _____

TALK ABOUT IT

1. What names are popular right now?
2. What girls' names call to your mind someone pretty? What boys' names call to your mind someone friendly?
3. Is your name a common or an uncommon name?
4. Do you like your name or would you prefer a different one?

BEFORE READING 11.3

Look at the title and the pictures. What do you think this reading will be about? Check (√) your answer.

_____ Good Names Around the World

_____ The Most Popular Names Around the World

_____ Raising Healthy Babies Around the World

_____ How Different Cultures Choose Names

Skim the reading. That is, read the first paragraph. Then, read the first line of each paragraph. Read the last paragraph. Was your guess right?

READING 11.3

Naming Names Around the World

1 In the sixteenth century, William Shakespeare, one of the most famous British authors, wrote "What's in a name? That which we call a rose by any other name would smell as sweet." By writing this, he was saying that a name isn't important. If we called a rose a different name, it wouldn't matter; it would still smell sweet. To William Shakespeare, a name wasn't important. However, to most parents of newborn babies, it's extremely important — not only what the name is, but also who chooses the name and when.

2 Different cultures had, and still have, different ways of deciding *who* names the baby. In some cultures, there is one special person who chooses the name — sometimes the mother, sometimes the father, sometimes an uncle, and so on. In some cultures, the parents decide together. In some places, the baby also has a "say" in the matter. In some parts of Africa, someone reads a list of names while the mother holds the baby. As soon as the baby sneezes, the person stops reading and the child gets the last name that was read. In parts of Malaysia, the parents follow the same practice but instead of waiting for the baby to sneeze, they wait for it to smile.

3 Different cultures also had, and still have, different ways of deciding *what* to name the baby. In some cultures, babies get a name describing their position in the family. In ancient Rome, for example, children had names like Quintus (fifth) or Octavia (eighth). In some cultures, parents name their babies for qualities they want them to have; for example, some American girls have the names Joy and Grace and some Mexican girls have the name Esperanza, which means "hope" in Spanish. In some cultures, babies' names come from religious books. In still other cultures, babies are named after relatives (dead or alive) or famous people.

4 Different cultures also had, and still have, different ways of deciding *when* to name a baby. In Bali, babies do not receive their official name until they are 110 days old. Until then, they only have nicknames. On the 110th day, there is a naming ceremony. Among some American Indian tribes, babies receive one name at birth, another at puberty, another when they do something noteworthy, and a final name when they retire in their old age.

5 Perhaps "a rose by any other name would smell as sweet," but try telling that to a new parent!!!

VOCABULARY

century	*n.*	hundred years (The sixteenth century equals 1500-1599.)
ancient	*adj.*	very old; of a long time ago
quality	*n.*	a personal characteristic
grace	*n.*	beauty in movement
official	*adj.*	describing something that is formally done (and usually recorded in a government office)
puberty	*n.*	the time when teenagers' bodies change from a childlike state to an adult state
noteworthy	*adj.*	worth attention

AFTER READING 11.3

1. **Another title of this article could be**

    ____ **a.** The Who, What, and When of Names   ____ **c.** How to Name A Child Correctly

    ____ **b.** The Naming Practices of People in Bali   ____ **d.** Why Names Are Not Important

2. **Match the paragraph with its main idea.**

Paragraph 2	There are different customs regarding when to name a baby.
Paragraph 3	There are different customs regarding what to name a baby.
Paragraph 4	There are different customs regarding who should name a baby.

3. **The article says that sometimes the baby has a "say" in its name. How many examples of this practice does the article mention? _____ Which countries are these examples from? _____ and _____ .**

4. **Paragraph three has examples of different ways to decide what to name the baby. One way is to name children for their position in the family. What are three other ways mentioned in paragraph three?**

    _____ _____ _____

5. **Write *T* if the sentence is true. Write *F* if the sentence is false.**

    ____ **a.** In Bali, babies only have nicknames until they are 110 days old.

    ____ **b.** Some American Indians get new names at different times in their life.

    ____ **c.** In all cultures, the mother decides what to name the newborn child.

LOOKING AT LANGUAGE

1. **"In some cultures, babies are named after relatives (dead or alive)." For example, Jack is the name of the newborn baby's grandfather. If the newborn baby is named after his grandfather, his name is Jack also.**
   Do people in your family name children after relatives? _____
   If so, do they name children after relatives who are dead or alive or either? _____

   _____

2. **William Shakespeare wrote in the 16th century. This means he wrote during the 1500s. What century are we in now? _____**
   What century did your great-grandparents live in? _____

3. **"Names are extremely important — not only what the name is, but also who chooses the name." In this sentence with "not only... but also," two things are important — both "what the name is" and "who chooses the name."**

    a. Not only is he rich but he is also handsome. This means he is both _____ and _____ .

    b. She not only plays the piano but also the violin. This means she plays both the _____ and the _____

CHALLENGE

How much do you know about children? If you can answer 7 or more of these questions correctly, you know quite a bit!

1. True or False?   Newborn boys, on the average, are heavier and larger than girls.

2. True or False?   Almost all newborns are born with blue or grey-blue eyes.

3. True or False?   Firstborn babies are usually bigger at birth than second or third born babies.

4. A newborn baby's head is about ____ the size of its entire body.

    ____ **a.** 1/8   ____ **b.** 1/4   ____ **c.** 1/2

5. True or False?   Babies do not have a good sense of smell.

6. True or False?   Newborns are colorblind (that is, they can't see the differences between colors).

7. At what age can almost all babies tell the difference between human voices and other sounds?

    ____ **a.** at birth   ____ **b.** at 1 week of age   ____ **c.** at 2 weeks of age

8. True or False?   On the average, boys begin to walk earlier than girls.

9. True or False?   The baby's brain grows more in the first year than in the second year.

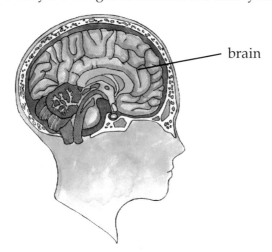

brain

10. What percent of births are twins?

    ____ **a.** about 1 in 90   ____ **b.** about 1 in 140   ____ **c.** about 1 in 180

QUOTES AND SAYINGS ABOUT CHILDREN

• *The child is father of the man.*

• *The apple never falls far from the tree.*

Which school subjects do you think are most interesting? What subjects do you think are least interesting? Rank the following subjects from 1 to 6 (with 1 being the least interesting to you and 6 being the most interesting).

biology class

math class

history class

chemistry class

literature class

music class

Talk to a classmate and ask these questions:

What subjects did you study in primary school?

What subjects did you (or do you) study in high school?

Was (or is) physical education a part of your educational curriculum?

Was (or is) art a part of your educational curriculum?

Was (or is) "home economics" or "family life" part of your educational curriculum?

READING 12.1

Monday, Janu...

Survey: **What was (or is) your favorite subject in school? What about your least favorite? Why?**

Marina Perez	**Pat Conn**	**Jeff Jones**	**Roberto Hernandez**	**Shinya Watanabe**	**May Chan**

"My favorite subject is math. I don't know why but it has always seemed easy to me. I actually think it's fun. It's like a puzzle. My favorite was algebra but I also liked geometry and trigonometry... and calculus, too. My least favorite class is history. Maybe it's the teachers but it seems so boring. It's just a lot of dates and wars."

"I used to love the science classes — all of them — biology, chemistry, geology, physics. I think I liked those classes because I felt that they helped me understand how the world works. For example, when I was a child, rain was a mystery to me. In my science class, I learned why it rains. I think the sciences clear up mysteries... but then there are always more mysteries to solve!!! What was my least favorite class? That was math. After learning the fundamentals, nothing else seemed very practical to me. I never saw how I could use it in my day to day life."

"My favorite subject was P.E. — physical education. I never stood out in other classes but in P.E., I was always one of the best. My least favorite class was English literature. I don't think I had the patience to sit and read then. I always felt restless in that class. Now, I feel differently. I've learned to appreciate good books and I love to take some quiet time to read."

"My favorite class was history — especially ancient history. People don't realize how advanced the ancient civilizations of Central America were. The Maya, for example, made important discoveries in math and created a very accurate calendar to predict the movement of the stars. Anyway, that's why I became an archaeologist— to learn more about this history. My least favorite class was P.E. I was a terrible athlete."

"My favorite class is astronomy. I'm so curious about other planets and the stars. If I could, I would love to be an astronaut. I feel like a real explorer when I learn about space because there's so much we don't know. Who knows — maybe there is life out there!! My least favorite subject is English. I wish I could learn it faster but I can't. It's so hard to remember all that vocabulary and grammar."

"I used to love my literature classes. Reading opened up a whole world for me. After I discovered books, I never again felt bored. I didn't always like everything we read in class but I always enjoyed discussing the ideas. Now, as an adult, I still read a lot. Books, to me, are like a faithful friend. What about my least favorite course? That was music. I guess I don't "have an ear" for music. I just don't appreciate most of it."

YOUR TURN

What was (or is) your favorite subject in school? Why?
What was (or is) your least favorite subject in school? Why?

UNDERSTANDING

1. **Fill in the chart to show each person's likes and dislikes.**

	Favorite Subject(s)	Least Favorite Subject(s)
Marina		
Pat		
Jeff		
Roberto		
Shinya		
May		

2. **Below are statements about school subjects. Write + if the sentence gives a reason to like the subject. Write − if the sentence gives a reason to dislike a subject.**

   __−__ a. It's boring.
   __+__ b. It's fun.
   ____ c. I am curious about the subject.
   ____ d. It's too hard.
   ____ e. I feel restless in that class.
   ____ f. Nothing seems very practical.
   ____ g. It helps me understand the world better.

3. **Write *T* if the statement is true; write *F* if the statement is false and correct it.**

   ____ a. Pat liked the sciences because they helped her understand the world better.
   ____ b. Pat didn't like math (after learning the basics) because it didn't seem useful to her.
   ____ c. Jeff didn't like English literature because he didn't like sitting and reading.
   ____ d. Jeff didn't like to read when he was a student and he still doesn't.
   ____ e. Roberto became an archaeologist because he was a terrible athlete.
   ____ f. May can't hear well; that's why she didn't like music.

THINK ABOUT IT

From what you read in the survey, which people have something in common? Why do you say that?

VOCABULARY PRACTICE: SCHOOL SUBJECTS

The words in the box are the names of subjects. Some are sciences; some are math areas; some are in an area called "the arts." Put the words in the correct category.

Sciences	Mathematics	Arts
_____	_____	_____
_____	_____	_____
_____	_____	_____
_____	_____	_____

algebra   astronomy
geology   chemistry
music   sculpture
calculus   biology
art history   geometry
trigonometry   drawing

THINK ABOUT IT

What subjects do you need to know in order to be an archaeologist?

79

READing 12.2

Schools are either public or private. Private schools sometimes advertise to attract new students. Look at these ads for private schools in the U.S. and Canada.

1.

RIVER VALLEY SCHOOL

A MORE MEANINGFUL HIGH SCHOOL EXPERIENCE IN PREPARATION FOR COLLEGE AND FOR LIFE

Accredited • Coed • Boarding/Day
Gr. 9-12 • Small Classes • Dedicated Staff
Sports • Arts • Computers •
Est. 1946 • Beautiful Rural Campus

WRITE OR CALL FOR FREE CATALOG

Ms. Florence Bates
12 Pasture Road
Boulder, Colorado 80996
1-800-888-5000
e-mail: flobates@rvs.com.

2.

Special Care for Special Children

Home environment for the mentally-handicapped child or adult. Opportunity for educational progress at any age — multiple recreational and social activities. A year round program with an active and full live-in lifestyle.

Est. 1983.
phone 1-800-900-7772
or write
THE JENNINGS HOME SCHOOL
Box 24, Greenwich, CT 06200
John R. Golden, M.D. Resident Physician

3.

EVERGREEN SCHOOL

A fully-accredited coeducational residential school that specializes in working with underachieving adolescents who are having problems at school and at home and who may be experiencing emotional difficulties.

• Counseling in personal growth and development
• Full college preparatory curriculum
• Year-round instruction grades 8-12
• Beautiful 250 acre mountain setting
• Warm, caring environment

P.O. Box 9, Olympia, WA 98550
(360) 555-1111
e-mail: egschool@wgn.com

4.

MT. VERNON MILITARY ACADEMY

BUILDING EXCELLENCE IN YOUNG MEN SINCE 1937.

• Grades 8-12, general and college-prep.
• All-boarding, all-male environment.
• Fully accredited. Small classes,weekly report cards.
• Excellent location near the Canadian Rockies.
• Affordable tuition.

Write or call:
P.O. Box 10
Branford, B.C.
3GM SHQ, Canada
Tel: 604-444-1500
Fax: 604-444-1505

VOCABULARY

accredited	*adj.*	describing a school which receives official approval because its educational curriculum meets official requirements
coed; coeducational	*adj.*	open to male and female students
boarding school	*n.*	a school where students live and eat on campus; a residential school
dedicated	*adj.*	describing someone who works very hard for an idea or place
staff	*n.*	the people who work at a place
est.	*v.*	established; founded; begun
rural	*adj.*	located in the country, not the city
campus	*n.*	the land and buildings of a school, college or university
mentally handicapped	*adj.*	describing a person who has a disability affecting the mind and thinking
progress	*n.*	improvement
recreation	*n.*	fun; amusement
underachieving	*adj.*	describing someone who isn't doing as well as he or she can
adolescents	*n.*	young teenagers (about 13-16)
counseling	*n.*	professional advice; guidance
college preparatory	*adj.*	describing a school that gets students ready for college/university
tuition	*n.*	the money a student pays to attend a school
faculty	*n.*	teaching staff
to enroll	*v.*	to register for a school or class

UNDERSTANDING

Look at the ads on page 80. Check the correct box or boxes.

	Ad#1	Ad #2	Ad #3	Ad #4
a. Which schools are "college prep" schools?				
b. Which school is not coed?				
c. Which school is the oldest?				
d. Which school specializes in mentally disabled adults and children?				
e. Which school specializes in teenagers who are having difficulties at home and school?				
f. Which school has a doctor as part of the staff?				

THINK ABOUT IT

Which schools do you think would be best for the following families?

a. The Kims have a daughter in the 11th grade. She's an excellent student and hopes to go to a good college. The school in ad # _____ would be best for her.

b. The Youngs have a 16-year-old son. He is intelligent but he is getting poor grades in school and getting into trouble after school. The school in ad # _____ or # _____ might be good for him.

TALK ABOUT IT

1. Ad #2 says the Jennings Home School has a "home environment." What do you think this means?

2. Why might parents send a child to a military academy, such as #4?

3. Why might parents send a child to a special school for the mentally handicapped, such as #2?

4. Are there similar private schools in most countries?

5. Do you know of any other kinds of private schools? If so, what kinds?

BEFORE READING 12.3

1. **Look at the title and the picture. What might this article be about?**

___ someone who looks like a young boy but is really an adult
___ someone who looks like an adult but is really a young boy
___ someone who looks like a young boy but doesn't always act like one
___ someone who looks like an adult but doesn't always act like one

Skim the article. Read the first paragraph and the first sentence of the other paragraphs. Read the last paragraph. Was your guess correct?

READING 12.3

Just a Kid? Look Again

1 He looks like a 12-year-old. He likes to play baseball and hockey and computer games with the neighborhood kids and his younger brother. According to his father, an Iranian immigrant to the U.S., "when you're around him a lot, one thing you notice is that he is just a kid."

2 Well, maybe not "just a kid." There aren't too many other small boys who can talk about a possible cure for Parkinson's Disease. And there aren't many other small boys who spend their summer vacations working in university laboratories. And there aren't many other small boys with I.Q.s of 200+, higher than Albert Einstein's I.Q. And there aren't many other 12-year-old college graduates.

3 Masoud Karkehabadi may be "just a kid" but he has the intelligence of a genius. He started speaking at the age of 8 months old. He began writing simple sentences by the time he was 2 and got his first computer the same year. When he was school age, his father wanted to send him to a private school; however, the schools turned Masoud down because they felt he was too advanced for his age. The father, then, hired private tutors for his son. By the time the child was 7, he had finished high school work. However, because Masoud was small for his age, his father decided to keep him home for two years instead of letting him go to college. During those years, he read on his own. At the age of 9, Masoud enrolled in college. Now 12, Masoud is a college graduate and planning to go to medical school.

4 Masoud is well aware of his special talent and says he wanted to find an "honorable way to donate it." When Masoud's hero, Mohammed Ali, the champion boxer, was diagnosed with Parkinson's disease, Masoud decided to dedicate his life to diseases of the mind, such as Parkinson's disease and Alzheimer's disease. "I want to find the cures for these diseases because I can then help millions of people," he said.

5 Masoud is not the youngest to graduate from college. (One boy, Michael Kearney, graduated at the age of 10 years and 5 months!) However, there is no doubt that he is special. "I feel I'm going to make a huge discovery," Masoud said recently at a fundraiser for Parkinson's disease research. The world wishes you luck, Masoud!

VOCABULARY

cure	*n.*	a remedy; something that makes a sick person better
laboratory	*n.*	a building or room containing scientific equipment
I.Q.	*n.*	a measure of intelligence
genius	*n.*	a person of very great and unusual ability
to turn someone down	*v.*	to refuse someone; to say "no" to someone
advanced	*adj.*	at a high level
to hire	*v.*	to employ; to pay someone money to do a job
tutor	*n.*	a person who helps someone with a school subject
talent	*n.*	a special skill or ability
honorable	*adj.*	respectable; showing or deserving respect
to donate	*v.*	to give (without expecting anything in return)
hero	*n.*	someone whom a person highly respects because of his/her good acts
there is no doubt	=	it is certain
discovery	*n.*	the finding of something which was unknown before

AFTER READING 12.3

1. Can you create a time line of Masoud Karkehabadi's life? Put the following information in the chart: "started speaking," "started writing sentences," "got his first computer," "started to study with tutors," "finished high school work," "started college," "graduated college."

born	2	4	6	8	10	12 years old

2. How is Masoud similar to other 12-year-olds? _____

_____

3. What is the main idea of paragraph 2?
   ____ **a.** Masoud is the same as other small boys.
   ____ **b.** Masoud is different from other small boys.
   ____ **c.** Masoud is aware of his special talents.
   ____ **d.** Masoud works in a laboratory.

4. Why did Masoud decide to study Parkinson's disease?
   ____ **a.** because his father has the disease   ____ **c.** because he wants to be famous
   ____ **b.** because his hero has the disease   ____ **d.** because he wants to be rich

5. Write *T* if the sentence is true; write *F* if the sentence is false and correct it.
   ____ **a.** Masoud lives in Iran.
   ____ **b.** Masoud is the youngest person to graduate from college.
   ____ **c.** Masoud went to private schools while he was growing up.
   ____ **d** Masoud is interested in doing medical research.

LOOKING AT LANGUAGE

1. The words "according to" mean "in the opinion of." Look at paragraph 1. Who believes that when you're around Masoud a lot, you notice that he is just a kid? _____

2. Look at the word that is circled. What is its reference? Draw an arrow to the word or words.

   a. When Masoud was school age, his father wanted to send (him) to a private school.
   b. The schools turned Masoud down because (they) felt (he) was too advanced for his age.
   c. Masoud is well aware of his special talent and says (he) wanted to find an "honorable way to donate (it.)"
   d. Masoud is not the youngest to graduate from college. (One boy, Michael Kearney, graduated at the age of 10 years and 5 months!) However, there is no doubt that (he) is special.

THINK ABOUT IT

Would you want to raise a child like Masoud? Why or why not?
Would you want to be a genius? Why or why not?

CHALLENGE

All of the words in the crossword puzzle are in Unit 12. Can you complete the puzzle?

<u>Across Clues</u>

3. A _____ school is a school where students live and eat on campus.
5. a child (informal language)
7. a person having extremely special and unusual talent or knowledge
9. Calculus, algebra, and geometry are three kinds of _____.
10. This describes a school that has both male and female students.
12. Masoud Karkehabadi wants to find a _____ for Parkinson's disease.
13. the study of ancient cultures and civilizations
14. the teaching staff of a school, college, or university

<u>Down Clues</u>

1. the buildings and land of a school, college or university
2. the great books and writings of a culture
4. a person whom one greatly respects because of the great things they do
6. the finding out of something new (something that was unknown before)
8. P.E. is an abbreviation for _____ education.
10. In some private schools, there are only 10 students in a _____. In some public schools, there may be more than 40.
11. workers at an organization, such as a school

QUOTES AND SAYINGS ABOUT EDUCATION	• *Knowledge is power.*
	• *You cannot teach an old dog new tricks.*

Money is a part of everyone's life. What are your views about money? Answer these questions by writing a number from 1-5 on the lines.

> 1=disagree completely
> 2=disagree somewhat
> 3=neither disagree nor agree
> 4=agree somewhat
> 5=agree completely

1. It's important to me to have a lot of money. _____

2. I don't need a lot of money; I just want to be comfortable. _____

3. Friends should not loan each other money. _____

4. It is important for a husband and wife to have similar spending habits. _____

5. I don't care about material things. _____

6. People should always be willing to lend money to family members. _____

7. If a restaurant undercharged me, I would tell them about their mistake. _____

8. If I found an expensive piece of jewelry, I would try to find the owner. _____

9. The difference between the rich and the poor is too large: there shouldn't be such a big difference. _____

10. I would rather receive a low salary from a job I love than a high salary from a job I hate. _____

 Sit in groups of four. Share your answers with each other. Talk about your reasons for giving your answers.

READING 13.1

Roni lost a ring last week and is not sure where she lost it. She wrote the following letters to try to locate it.

Roni Lebauer
222 Main St.
Laguna Beach, CA 92651

July 2

Holiday Hotel
256 Pine St.
San Francisco, CA 90035

To whom it may concern,

Last Tuesday and Wednesday, I stayed at your hotel in room #306. While I was there, I may have lost an antique ring. The ring is made of silver and has a small ruby and a small pearl in it. I would appreciate it if you could notify your housekeeping staff and let them know that I am offering a reward for the ring's return. My telephone number is 423-2796.

Thank you for your assistance in this matter.

Sincerely,

Roni Lebauer
Roni Lebauer

July 2

Dear Sue,

Did I by any chance lose my ring at your house when I was visiting last Thursday? I think you know the ring I'm talking about. I wear it pretty often. It's the silver one with a pearl and a ruby.

I would really appreciate it if you would take a look around the living room and kitchen. (I don't think I went anywhere else in your house.) If you find it, please call right away. Thanks so much!

Love,
Roni

Roni also put an ad in the newspaper.

pearl

oyster

LOST & FOUND

Lost Ring! Reward for Return!
Lost between 6/25 and 7/1 in Laguna Beach or San Francisco. Women's silver ring w/small ruby & pearl. **Call 423-2796.**

VOCABULARY

antique	*adj.*	old (e.g., a piece of furniture or jewelry)
to notify someone	*v.*	to give someone information
to offer something	*v.*	to be willing to give something if someone wants it
reward	*n.*	something given in return for a special action or service
assistance	*n.*	help
matter	*n.*	something which needs attention
by any chance	=	possibly

UNDERSTANDING

1. Which might be Roni's ring? Check the correct picture.

2. Write *T* if the sentence is true; write *F* if the sentence is false and correct it. (Sometimes the answer is not stated directly in the letters, but you can make an educated guess from the information you have.)

_____ **a.** Roni stayed 2 nights at the Holiday Hotel.

_____ **b.** Roni spent 2 nights at Sue's house.

_____ **c.** Sue lives in either Laguna Beach or San Francisco.

_____ **d.** Roni doesn't usually wear rings.

_____ **e.** Sue knows Roni's phone number.

_____ **f.** Roni doesn't know the name of the manager of the Holiday Hotel.

_____ **g.** Roni isn't sure where she lost the ring.

_____ **h.** The ring is new.

TALK ABOUT IT

1. **Do you lose things frequently or infrequently?**
2. **What was the last thing you lost? How did you lose it?**
3. **Did you find it?**

VOCABULARY PRACTICE: MONEY AND THE BANK

Using vocabulary shown in the pictures at the right, fill in the blanks in the sentences

1. At the bank, you will probably see these two people:
a _____ and a _____.

2. When you travel and you don't want to carry cash, you can pay with a _____ or _____.
Usually, you can't pay with a personal check when you are traveling.

3. When you want to save money, you open an account at the bank. When you want to put money in your account, you fill out a deposit slip. When you want to take money out of your account, you fill out a withdrawal slip. Every month, you receive a statement from your bank. The statement shows your _____ and _____ and at the end, it shows your _____.

4. If you want to send money through the mail, you should send a _____, not cash.

monthly statement

MANSON · BANK
STATEMENT OF ACCOUNT •

DEPOSIT	WITHDRAWAL	BALANCE

Diners Club International

credit card

security guard

teller

personal check

traveler's check

money or cash

READING 13.2

Save the Children is a charity which works with families and communities around the world to help bring about improvements in children's lives. This ad is in many magazines.

Help Her. Write Now.

To a desperately poor girl or boy, Save the Children sponsorship can mean at least one nutritious daily meal, basic health care, education—even self-help programs that benefit an entire community.

Whatever a child needs most, your gift of $20 a month—just 65¢ a day—can help provide. Not as a direct handout but by being combined with the monthly gifts of other caring sponsors.

There's another kind of help that sponsors provide that's even more personal: writing a short note every now and then. This simple expression of caring and encouragement can do wonders for a child's self-esteem. It's also the way to establish an ongoing, two-way relationship that will mean so much to you as well.

You can begin right here by simply writing a few words. We'll quickly match you with a waiting child. Then, while we're sending your note to your special girl or boy, we'll mail you a welcome kit containing your sponsored child's photo and personal history. And as you two are getting to know each other, your first monthly gift will be making its way to benefit your new friend.

Writing just a note is a very loving way to begin sponsorship. Please, open your heart and touch a fragile life, right now.

How Save the Children Funds are Spent
- 83.3% Program Services
- 9.3% Fundraising
- 7.4% Management & General

Just say "Hello."
We'll translate your message if necessary and rush it to the child who most urgently needs a caring friend like you.

Yes, It's the Right Thing to Do.

I prefer to sponsor a ❑ boy ❑ girl ❑ either, in the area I've checked below.
❑ Where the need is greatest ❑ Africa ❑ American Indian ❑ Asia
❑ Middle East ❑ Latin America ❑ United States
Age range: ❑ 2-7   ❑ 8 and older (optional)

Name _____ Phone (_____) _____
Address _____ Apt. _____
City _____ State _____ Zip _____

©1994 Serve the Children Federation.

Save the Children
50 Wilton Road, CT 06880

VOCABULARY

charity	n.	an organization that gives help to the poor
to sponsor	v.	to take some or all responsibility (for a person or group)
to benefit	v.	to be good for
entire	adj.	whole
community	n.	group of people living in the same neighborhood
to provide something	v.	to give something useful
handout	n.	something (such as food) one gives for free to someone who is poor
to combine	v.	to put together with
every now and then	adv.	sometimes
to express something	v.	to show one's feelings in words or in other ways
to do wonders	v.	to do great things
self-esteem	n.	feeling of confidence and respect for oneself
fragile	adj.	delicate; easily hurt
funds	n.	money
contribution	n.	donation; money given to a charity

UNDERSTANDING

Look back at page 88.

1. What does "Save the Children" do? Check (√) all the correct answers.

    _____ It tries to improve children's lives.
    _____ It gives direct handouts to the children.
    _____ It combines contributions from many sponsors.
    _____ It helps people only in the U.S.A.
    _____ It makes sure that letters from sponsors get to children.
    _____ It helps children eat better and get better health care and education.

2. What does "Save the Children" want sponsors to do? Check all the correct answers.

    _____ It wants sponsors to make a monthly donation.
    _____ It wants sponsors to write letters to the children.
    _____ It wants sponsors to visit the children.

3. What percent of the contributions to "Save the Children" go to the charity work
    itself (and not to advertising costs or management costs)? _____ %

4. If someone wants to be a sponsor, what choices does she have? Check all the
    correct answers.

    _____ She can choose whether to sponsor a boy or girl.
    _____ She can choose where to sponsor a child.
    _____ She can choose the age range of the child she wants to sponsor.

THINK ABOUT IT

Is this a good advertisement? Why or why not?

Why does "Save the Children" want sponsors to write to the children?

Do you give money to any charities? If so, what kind?

BEFORE READING 13.3

Following is a short newspaper article. It appeared in *The Register*, a California newspaper. The article tells about a hotel housekeeper who found jewelry while she was cleaning a hotel room — jewelry worth $100,000. Read the article to see what the housekeeper did with the jewels!!!

READING 13.3

Hotel housekeeper makes sparkling discovery at work

1 When Shirley Wagner of Hollywood Hills checked out of the Newport Beach Marriott Hotel & Tennis Club this past week, she forgot something — jewelry worth $100,000.

2 Meanwhile, hotel housekeeper Maria Jimenez was making the rounds that morning to clean, dust and vacuum the rooms. As she dusted off the air-conditioning unit in Wagner's room, she came across a small cloth bag behind the drapes. Opening the pouch, Jimenez was stunned to see a collection of diamonds, emeralds and gold chains.

3 Jimenez, almost fearful to leave the room, called her supervisor from a phone in the room. Unable to reach the supervisor, she quickly walked to the security office where the items were logged in, said Leanne DuPay, a Marriott spokeswoman.

4 Wagner, who was at home unpacking from the weekend get-away was stricken with panic as she realized her jewelry was missing. She called the hotel and was told the items were there.

5 Wagner, who apparently carries the jewelry for fear they'd get lost in the next big earthquake, plans to give Jimenez a $400 reward, DuPay said. She added that the hotel plans to give the five-year employee a commendation and will name her employee of the month.

VOCABULARY

sparkling	*adj.*	describing something that shines (like sun on water)
to check out of a hotel	*v.*	to pay and leave a hotel after staying there
meanwhile	*adv.*	at the same time
to make the rounds	*v.*	to make a regular set of visits to a number of people, rooms, etc.
to come across something	*v.*	to find something
drapes	*n.*	curtains that cover the windows down to the floor
stunned	*adj.*	shocked; very surprised
emeralds	*n.*	clear, green, expensive jewels
supervisor	*n.*	boss
to log something in	*v.*	to write something down in a book (for a record)
spokesperson	*n.*	a person who officially speaks for a group or organization
to be stricken with panic	*v.*	to feel fear and nervousness suddenly
earthquake	*n.*	a sudden, sometimes strong, movement of the earth
commendation	*n.*	an official honor one gets for doing a good act

AFTER READING 13.3

1. Did Maria Jimenez, the housekeeper, do what you expected?
2. What happened first? Second? Third? Number the pictures from *1* to *7*, with *1* being the first event, and so on.

3. Why did Wagner take those jewels with her to the hotel?
   ____ She was afraid someone would steal them if she left them home alone.
   ____ She was afraid she would lose them in an earthquake at home.
   ____ She wanted to wear them that night.
   ____ She wanted to sell them.

LOOKING AT LANGUAGE

1. When you are reading long sentences, try to find the main sentence — the main subject and verb. Often, the part of the sentence surrounded by commas is extra. In the sentence that follows, the main sentence is underlined.

   Example: <u>Jimenez</u>, almost fearful to leave the room, <u>called her supervisor from a phone.</u>

   Underline the main sentence in each of the following.

   a. Wagner, who was at home unpacking from the weekend getaway, was stricken with panic.
   b. Wagner, who apparently carries the jewelry for fear they'd get lost in the next big earthquake, plans to give Jimenez a $400 reward.

2. The word "meanwhile" connects two things that happen at the same time. Reread the first two paragraphs. What was happening while Maria Jimenez was making her rounds?

   _____

3. Can you guess the meaning of the underlined word?

   Jimenez came across a small cloth bag behind the drapes. Opening the <u>pouch</u>, she was stunned to see a collection of jewels.

THINK ABOUT IT

1. Did Jimenez do the right thing? Did Jimenez do the smart thing?
2. Was Jimenez' reward from Wagner and the hotel good enough?

CHALLENGE

Amy, Barbara, Charles, David and George went shopping yesterday. They all went to the same department store and each person only made one purchase. However, they bought different things and spent different amounts of money. From the clues below, can you figure out what each person bought, what floor each person went to, and how much he or she spent? (Hint: check p. 72 to see which names are women's names and which names are men's names.)

1. There are four floors in the department store. The first floor has clothes and jewelry. The second floor has appliances and electrical items. The third floor has furniture. The fourth floor has toys and sports equipment.

2. Only Charles and Amy bought something on the same floor.
3. The woman who bought the stuffed animal spent $6.
4. One person bought a coffeemaker for $15.
5. Amy spent 1/4 as much as David.
6. Charles bought a small TV.
7. The earrings were $22.
8. The most expensive item was $250 and it wasn't the table.

If you think you know the answer, fill in the blanks below.

Amy   bought the _____ for $_____ on the _____ floor.

Barbara   bought the _____ for $_____ on the _____ floor.

Charles   bought the _____ for $_____ on the _____ floor.

David   bought the _____ for $_____ on the _____ floor.

George   bought the _____ for $_____ on the _____ floor.

QUOTES AND SAYINGS ABOUT MONEY

- *Money is the root of all evil.*
- *Money is a terrible master but an excellent servant.*

Complete the sentences with information about yourself.

1. When I was younger, I lived with _____.
2. When I was a child, I used to love to _____.
3. When I was a child, I used to hate to _____.
4. When I was younger, I used to _____ but now I don't.
5. When I was younger, I wanted to be a _____.
6. When I was younger, I hated to eat _____.

Fill in the blanks with *always*, *often*, *sometimes*, *rarely*, **or** *never*.

7. When I was younger, I _____ got into trouble.
8. When I was younger, I _____ fought with other children.
9. When I was younger, I _____ played by myself.
10. When I was younger, I _____ played outdoors.

Share your answers with a classmate. Then, tell the rest of the class something you learned about your classmate's childhood.

 **READING 14.1**

Survey: **Tell me about something you used to do but don't do anymore. Why did you stop?**

Jim Miller Retired	**Carla Gomez** Homemaker	**Michael Chen** University Student	**Linda Lane** Engineer	**Arturo Cortes** Businessman	**Mary Moore** Student

"I grew up in a rural area and so my friends and I used to spend a lot of time playing outdoors. I remember going to a lake nearby and swimming and fishing. There was a rope near the water and we used to hang on the rope and swing ourselves into the water. We had a lot of fun. Now that I live in a city, I'm not near a lake like that. Too bad. Those were great times!"

"I used to read a lot — mysteries, fiction, non-fiction, biographies — almost anything. Sometimes, I would read 3 or 4 books a week. Now it's impossible. I'm lucky if I get to read a newspaper or magazine. I have 2 kids — Carlos is 3 and Norma is 6 months old. Being a mother is a full-time job. When one child is sleeping, usually the other one needs my attention."

"I used to take piano lessons but I stopped last year. I don't think I ever really enjoyed the piano but I had to take lessons because my parents wanted me to learn a musical instrument. Maybe in the future, I'll be happy that I know how to play but right now, I'm happy that I don't have to practice. I have better things to do with my time – like spending time with my girlfriend!"

"I used to be really athletic. I played on a tennis team. I ran every day. I lifted weights. Then, everything changed the day a drunk driver hit my car. Ever since that accident, I've needed to use a wheelchair. Obviously, I can't run...but I do still play tennis and I still do lift weights. The accident changed my life but it won't keep me away from sports and exercise."

"I used to smoke — 3 packs a day. I started when I was an adolescent. I thought it was "cool." I wanted to be part of the group. I wanted to look older. By the time I turned 30, I could feel the effects of 15 years of smoking. When I exercised, I would get out of breath easily. I also worried because my wife was pregnant and I didn't want my child to grow up around smoke. Researchers say that secondhand smoke really hurts kids. So I stopped — cold turkey — on my 31st birthday. It wasn't easy but I'm glad I did it."

"I used to fight a lot with my younger sister. She's two years younger than I am and she always used to want to follow me everywhere. It bothered me because I felt like I always had a shadow. Now, things are different. Because we're both older, I'm finding that I really enjoy her company. Of course, she has her own friends now and her own interests. I think of her now as my best friend!"

YOUR TURN

Talk about something you used to do but don't do anymore. Why did you stop?

UNDERSTANDING

1. The pictures below show past activities of the people surveyed on page 94. Write the correct name under the picture.

_____   _____   _____   _____   _____   _____

2. Complete the sentences with information from the survey.

   a. Jim changed because _____.

   b. Carla changed because _____.

   c. Michael changed because _____.

   d. Linda changed because _____.

   e. Arturo changed because _____ and because

   _____.

   f. Mary changed because _____.

3. Who doesn't want to start doing his or her old activity again?
   (Check as many as are correct.)

   ____ a. Mary   ____ b. Michael   ____ c. Arturo

VOCABULARY PRACTICE: CHILDHOOD TOYS

Which of the following toys did you use to play with when you were a child? Which toys didn't you like? Make sentences using this form: "When I was _____ years old, I used to play with _____ s." or "When I was a child, I never liked to play with _____ s."

blocks   jigsaw puzzle   jump rope   ball   tricycle

electronic games   crayons   stuffed animals   doll   bicycle

roller blades   doll house   toy truck   skateboard   toy gun

READING 14.2

Did you use to go to movies when you were younger? What kind of movies did you enjoy?

Following are descriptions of some movies. Many are available in video stores. The stars next to the title show a movie critic's opinion of the movie.

★★★★ = Excellent
★★★ = Good
★★ = Average
★ = Poor

Assassins
★

(1995)   Sylvester Stallone
         Antonio Banderas

Two hit men search for an important computer disk (worth millions of dollars in reward money).
2 hrs.

Home Alone 2: Lost in New York
★★★

(1992)   McCaulay Culkin

Left behind by his family, the boy hero lands in New York City and fights against two robbers.
2 hrs.

The Lion, The Witch, and the Wardrobe
★★★

(1979)   Animated

Children go through a closet to get to the magic land called Narnia.
1 hr. 35 mins.

Beverly Hills Cop
★★★

(1984)   Eddie Murphy

A detective drives to Los Angeles to show cops how to catch a killer.
1 hr. 45 mins.

King Kong
★★★★

(1933)   Fay Wray

Giant ape escapes and carries a blonde up the Empire State Building.
2 hrs.

The Train Robbers
★★

(1973)   John Wayne

A widow hires a man to find the gold that her dead husband robbed.
2 hrs.

The Big Store
★★

(1941)   The Marx Brothers

Groucho, Chico, and Harpo cause trouble in a department store where Groucho works as a security guard.
1 hr. 24 mins

A Kiss Before Dying
★★★

(1956)   Robert Wagner

A college student kills his rich girlfriend and tries to date her sister who does not know he is the killer.
1 hr. 24 mins.

True Lies
★★★

(1994) Arnold Schwarzenegger
        Jamie Lee Curtis

A spy hides his dangerous work from his wife (who thinks he is a computer salesman).
2 hrs. 15 mins.

Chaplin
★★★

(1992)   Robert Downey Jr.

The story of silent film star, Charlie Chaplin, begins with poverty in London and ends in Hollywood.
2 hrs. 24 mins.

A League of Their Own
★★★

(1992)   Madonna

A women's baseball team begins in 1943.
2 hrs. 8 mins.

Yours, Mine, and Ours
★★★

(1968)   Lucille Ball

A widow with eight children meets, dates, and weds a widowed man with 10 children.
1 hr. 51 mins.

VOCABULARY

movie critic	n.	a person who sees movies and writes articles about their good and bad points
poor	adj.	not good
assassin	n.	a killer
hit man	n.	a hired killer
reward	n.	money given to the person who finds and returns a lost object
cop	n.	(informal) policeman or woman
poverty	n.	the state of being poor
silent	adj.	without sound
star	n.	a famous person (such as a movie star or a rock star)
robber	n.	a person who takes things from a store or a person without asking or paying
ape	n.	a large monkey
to date	v.	to have a special meeting with someone you are interested in romantically
wardrobe	n.	a piece of furniture used for hanging clothes
magic	adj.	having strange, secret, or unnatural powers or abilities
animated	adj.	like a cartoon; a film that uses drawings, not actors
spy	n.	a person whose job is the discovery of secrets
widow	n.	a woman whose husband has died (a widower is a man whose wife has died)

SCANNING

How many questions can you answer in one minute?

1. When was "Home Alone 2" made? _____
2. How long is "Assassins"? _____
3. How many stars did "A Kiss Before Dying" get? _____
4. What do 2 stars mean? _____
5. Who is the star of "Yours, Mine, and Ours"? _____
6. When was "King Kong" made? _____
7. How long is "Chaplin"? _____
8. How many stars did "The Big Store" get? _____
9. What do 4 stars mean? _____
10. Who is the star of "A League of Their Own"? _____

UNDERSTANDING

Look at the movie descriptions on p. 96. Which movie matches each picture? Write the name next to the picture.

_____

_____

THINK ABOUT IT

1. **Which of the movies on p. 96 might be best for very young children?**
2. **Which of the movies might be violent?**
3. **Which of the movies might be funny?**
4. **Which of the movies is based on a true story?**
5. **Which of the movies would you like to see?**

97

BEFORE READING 14.3

Charlie Chaplin is known all over the world. Because so many of his films are silent, film-goers can appreciate his films without understanding the English language. Have you ever seen a Charlie Chaplin film? What do you know about Charlie Chaplin?

READING 14.3

Chaplin, Charlie 1889-1977

Charlie Chaplin: The Little Tramp

Born:	*4/16/1889 in England*
Childhood:	*A difficult childhood. Father left family. Mother frequently in the hospital with mental illness. Years of poverty, especially between 1894-8.*
Family:	*First marriage to Mildred Harris, who was 16 years old at the time. One child died 3 days after birth.*
	Second marriage to Lita Grey, who was 16 years old at the time, in 1924. Two children.
	Third marriage to Paulette Goddard who was 24 years old at the time, in 1936.
	Fourth marriage to Oona O'Neill, who was 18 years old at the time, in 1943. Eight children.
Movies:	*More than 80 movies including The Tramp (1915), A Dog's Life (1918), The Kid (1921), City Lights (1931), Modern Times (1936), The Great Dictator (1940)*
Awards:	*Received special Academy Award in 1972. Knighted in 1975.*
Quote:	*"To work is to live — and I love to live." (6/30/76)*
Died:	*12/25/1977. (Two men robbed his body on March 1, 1978, but police found it 17 days later.)*

Memories of Charlie

Claire Bloom, an actress, remembers working with Chaplin. Here's what she said.

- *"Chaplin was a perfectionist. When he was working and was angry, everybody knew it. He never raised his voice. He was just very obviously displeased."*
- *"He was always fascinating to watch. There were things he did that...I don't really know how he did them. He could do amazing tricks with his umbrella and hat — make them fly and, in the case of his hat, come back to rest on his head."*
- *"Chaplin was very punctual and meticulous in everything. He was meticulous about his dress, his house, his films, his manners... neatness in movement and speech. His speech was quite interesting because it was old-fashioned."*
- *"Almost everybody knew who he was...I remember once — when Oona was away during the winter...Charlie said "Let's go for a walk through London." And that was when we went to Covent Garden...and as he passed, they tipped their hats. This was workingmen saluting someone they had known all their lives. They knew he was one of them."*

Charlie Chaplin ▸ Claire Bloom

VOCABULARY

tramp	*n.*	a person with no home or job, who moves from place to place
dictator	*n.*	a ruler who has complete power
award	*n.*	a prize or money which is given to honor someone officially
to be knighted	*v.*	to receive the title "Sir" from the Queen or King of England
perfectionist	*n.*	someone who wants everything to be perfect

obviously	adv.	clearly; noticeably
fascinating	adj.	very interesting
amazing	adj.	causing surprise because of how wonderful something is
tricks	n.	acts done to amaze, entertain, or surprise people
punctual	adj.	on time
meticulous	adj.	very neat and exact
manners	n.	the way or style of doing something
speech	n.	the way one talks
to tip one's hat	v.	to lift one's hat to say hello
to salute	v.	to wave one's hand to greet (to say "hello"), especially without a word

AFTER READING 14.3

1. **Write _T_ if the sentence is true. Write _F_ if the sentence is false and correct it.**

    ____ **a.** Chaplin's childhood was easy.
    ____ **b.** Chaplin's mother had no health problems.
    ____ **c.** Chaplin was married 4 times.
    ____ **d.** According to Claire Bloom, Chaplin spoke loudly when he was angry.
    ____ **e.** According to Claire Bloom, Chaplin did not care much about his appearance.
    ____ **f.** According to Claire Bloom, when Chaplin walked in the streets, no one paid attention to him.

2. **What happened after Chaplin's death?**

    ____ **a.** His wife gave birth to another child.   ____ **c.** Someone took his body from the cemetery.
    ____ **b.** He received another award.   ____ **d.** He was knighted.

3. **According to Claire Bloom, why did the workingmen salute Chaplin in the park?**

    ____ **a.** They were good friends when they were children in the same neighborhood.
    ____ **b.** They felt that he understood their lives.
    ____ **c.** They liked his clothes.

LOOKING AT LANGUAGE

1. **Claire Bloom said. "Chaplin was a perfectionist. When he was working and was angry, everybody knew it. He never raised his voice. He was just very obviously displeased."**
    The suffix -ist means _a person_. It is similar to the suffix -er.
    The prefix dis- means _not_. It is similar to the prefix un-.
    Check the words which have the suffix -ist meaning _a person_.
    ____ typist   ____ list   ____ wrist   ____ receptionist   ____ pianist

    Check the words which have the prefix dis- meaning _not_.
    ____ disagree   ____ dishes   ____ disbelieve   ____ discontinue   ____ dislike

2. **Look at the word that is circled. What is its reference? Draw an arrow to the word or words.**
    a. His first marriage was to Mildred Harris, (who) was 16 years old at the time.
    b. When he was working and was angry, everybody knew (it.)
    c. He could do amazing tricks with his umbrella and hat — make (them) fly.

THINK ABOUT IT

Chaplin said "To work is to live — and I love to live." What did he mean?

CHALLENGE

Can you find 15 words from the chapter relating to movies and childhood? You may find the words vertically (↕), horizontally (↔), or diagonally (↗) or (↘). A word list is given below the puzzle, but first try to find the words without the list. It's more of a challenge.

S	C	A	M	O	V	I	E	S	I	S
T	R	A	J	B	L	O	C	K	S	I
A	A	N	C	U	A	R	S	A	T	B
M	Y	N	R	D	M	E	T	T	R	I
L	O	V	I	B	O	P	A	E	A	C
P	N	V	T	M	A	L	R	B	A	Y
U	S	M	I	T	A	L	L	O	R	C
Z	I	F	C	O	T	T	L	A	P	L
T	R	I	C	Y	C	L	E	R	U	E
R	E	L	E	O	O	A	Z	D	Z	N
I	T	M	P	U	Z	Z	L	E	Z	M

blocks, puzzle, skateboard, film, jumprope, ball, star, animated, tricycle, bicycle, toy, crayons, doll, critic, movies

---

QUOTES AND SAYINGS ABOUT MEMORIES

- *"Every man's memory is his private literature."*
  -Aldous Huxley

- *"Nothing can bring back the hour*
  Of splendor in the grass, of the glory of the
  flower."
  -William Wordsworth

I walked into my dark office and immediately saw the blinking light on my answering machine. "Oh well. Another busy day," I thought to myself. Then, I remembered that I should be thankful for the blinking light. It was my own business after all — Ann Ryan, Private Detective — and I needed the work.

Cup of tea in hand, I sat down to listen to the message.

"Ann?"

I recognized the voice but wasn't sure who it was.

"This is Lena. I can't remember when we last spoke but I need to talk to you soon. I have a problem and I'm hoping you can help. Would you call me back as soon as possible? My number is still the same — 555-7409."

Lena Dunn. My best friend in high school. We hadn't seen each other for 10 years or more.

I dialed her number right away.

Lena answered on the first ring. She sounded depressed. When she asked me to meet her at her house, I agreed. I knew the address. As high school friends, we used to spend lots of time there.

The neighborhood looked older and dirtier than I remembered it. As I drove around, memories came back to me. I passed the park where we used to play volleyball. I passed our high school. I remembered the hours we spent in classes — history, chemistry, math. I remembered how much we hated chemistry.

As I turned the corner, I saw Lena's house. The paint looked new but the yard needed work.

Lena opened the door before I rang the bell.

The house was just as I remembered it. I almost expected Lena's mother to walk in and welcome me even though I knew that her mother had died earlier that year. Lena lived by herself now.

I looked around. The furniture was the same. Even the pictures on the wall.

At that moment, I heard the train go by. I smiled to myself. I remembered how the train used to go by every 20 minutes. At first, it bothered me but like the rest of the Dunn family, I soon forgot about it.

"Nothing has changed," I said.

Lena smiled a little sadly, "Nothing."

After some coffee and small talk, Lena started to tell me why she needed my help.

"You know that my mom died about 9 months ago," she said. I nodded my head. "I miss her so much. The house seems empty without her. Anyway, my mother always talked about writing a will but she never did it. She said she didn't want to think about death. I didn't want to think about it either, so I didn't say anything."

"One day, however, she called me into her room — that room, over there — and asked me to bring a tape recorder. For some reason, she wanted to tape her wishes, not write them. I think she talked into that tape recorder for about an hour. She didn't miss anything — the bank accounts, the furniture, the jewelry, the car, the pictures, the house. She was very clear that she wanted my uncles to get some small things and she wanted me to get everything else."

"The problem is that my uncles don't believe the tape is real. They think I'm trying to cheat them. How can I prove that it's real? That's why I need your help."

"Can I listen to the tape?" I asked.

Lena nodded her head. "It's long. About an hour. But please listen if you think it can help you."

Lena brought in the tape recorder and I sat back in the chair. If I closed my eyes, I could imagine that her mom was standing in front of me. The recording was so clear. No noise. Just her mother's voice. The hour passed by quickly.

When the tape was finished, I looked at Lena.

"I can't help you," I said.

"Why?"

"There's something wrong with this tape," I answered.

VOCABULARY

a will	*n.*	a legal paper stating a person's wishes after his or her death
blinking	*adj.*	going on and off
small talk	*n.*	talk about unimportant things
to cheat	*v.*	to act in a dishonest or unfair way to get something
to prove	*v.*	to show that something is true

UNDERSTANDING

Look at the pictures below. Number the pictures from *1-7* to show the events in the story.

DO IT

Work in groups of 3 to read this story out loud to the class. One person is the narrator. One person is the detective. One person is Lena. If you are male, change the detective's name to Arnold Ryan or change Lena's name to Len Dunn. The narrator can be a male or female.

THINK ABOUT IT

What was wrong with the tape?

UNIT 16 Congratulations! You're Hired!

Elena, Saman, and Thanh are teenagers. They need to think about what work they want to do in the future. Read what they say about themselves.

Elena

"I love working in a creative way. I don't think I can sit at a desk all day. I also don't think I want to work regular hours. I don't want to start every day at 8 and end every day at 6. I would prefer to make my own hours or change hours each week. Sometimes, I even like to work in the middle of the night. My teachers say I'm good at writing. I can work alone or with people; it doesn't matter to me."

"I really want a job where I can spend some time or all of the time outdoors. My teachers say I'm very coordinated and have good mechanical ability. When I was a child, I loved to build things and then take them apart and then rebuild them!!! I work pretty well with other people."

Saman

Thanh

"I want a part-time job that helps people. I don't care about just making money. I want to feel that my job does something good for people. My teachers say that I work very well with others. That's important to me. After school, I tutor some younger children in math. I'm also good at sports. I've thought about being a doctor or nurse but I can't stand the sight of blood!!"

Work in groups of three to decide two possible jobs for Elena, Saman, and Thanh.

Elena might want to become a _____ or a _____ because
_____ .

Saman might want to become a _____ or a _____ because
_____ .

Thanh might want to become a _____ or a _____ because
_____ .

Write 2 sentences about possible jobs for yourself.
Example: *I could be a good mechanic because I know a lot about cars.*

I could be a good _____ because _____ .
I could be a good _____ because _____ .

READING 16.1

Thanh saw the following job ad in a newspaper. Why might she be good for this job?

WANTED:

LIFEGUARD

for neighborhood pool. 20 hours a week beginning **June 1st**.
Call **775-1290** for application and information about hours and pay.

Thanh called for an application. When she sent her application, she also sent the following cover letter:

Thanh Nguyen
267 Orange Ave.
New York, N.Y. 10011
May 12, 1999

Luisa Ruiz, Director
Third Street Community Center
201 Third Street
New York, New York 10022

Dear Ms. Ruiz,

I am very interested in applying for the lifeguard position at the Third Street Community Center. I think that my experience and my training would make me an excellent lifeguard at your pool.

I have a lot of experience working with children. Currently, after school, I tutor 10 and 11-year-olds in math. Last summer, I was an assistant at a childcare center. One of my duties there was to supervise children in the playground.

I am a very good swimmer. I'm on the swimming team of my school and my teachers say that I'm a "natural" athlete. Not only do I swim well, but I also can teach swimming. I've taught my two younger brothers and a few family friends how to swim. I have training and certificates in water safety and lifesaving techniques.

I consider myself to be a responsible person. If I agree to do something, I always do it. I am punctual and hardworking. (I am always willing to do extra work when it is necessary.)

If you would like references, you can call my high school teacher, Ms. Lane, at 231-9658. You can also call Mr. Jones, my tutoring supervisor, at 915-8709. I look forward to meeting with you.

Sincerely,

Thanh Nguyen

Thanh Nguyen

VOCABULARY

lifeguard	*n.*	a job where one makes sure swimmers at a pool or beach are safe
to apply for a position	*v.*	to ask to be considered for a job
experience	*n.*	knowledge or skills that one gets from doing something
training	*n.*	education in job-related skills
currently	*adv.*	now; presently
tutor	*n.*	to teach a very small group informally
duty	*n.*	a responsibility of a job
responsible	*adj.*	reliable; dependable; trustworthy
punctual	*adj.*	always on time
references	*n.*	information given to a possible employer about a job applicant's work and personality
supervisor	*n.*	a person who watches and manages the work of others

UNDERSTANDING

1. **What position is Thanh applying for? Check the correct picture.**

2. **Write *T* if the sentence is true; write *F* if the sentence is false.**

   _____ **a.** Mr. Jones is a tutor.
   _____ **b.** If someone falls in the water and he can't swim, Thanh knows how to save him.
   _____ **c.** Thanh knows how to teach people how to swim.
   _____ **d.** Thanh thinks she is a reliable person.

3. **The following information is not in the letter. However, you can *infer* whether this information is probably true or probably false. (*Inferring* means you make a reasonable guess using the information you have.) Write *PT* if the sentence is *probably true*; write *PF* if the sentence is *probably false*.**

   _____ **a.** Thanh is good at math.
   _____ **b.** Thanh knows how to play other sports.
   _____ **c.** Thanh thinks Ms. Lane and Mr. Jones will say good things about her.
   _____ **d.** Thanh worked as a lifeguard before.

VOCABULARY PRACTICE: JOBS AND DUTIES

Fill in the blanks with a word from the box on the right. You will not use all the words.

1. My cat seems very tired and is not eating. I should take my cat to a _____.
2. I need to find books and articles about Greenland. I should talk to a _____.
3. You might want to go to that new restaurant. I've heard that the _____ prepares very delicious food.
4. I'm thinking about building a house. Can you recommend a good _____?
5. Our _____ told us that our business is losing money. She says we're spending more money than we're receiving.
6. He's not a very good _____. He doesn't take clear messages and he doesn't sound business-like on the phone.
7. When you're planning a trip, you might want to talk to a _____. She can arrange transportation, lodging, tours, and more.
8. Take your prescription to the _____ and he will get you your medicine.

architect
librarian
security guard
pharmacist
travel agent
reporter
accountant
receptionist
veterinarian
chef
plumber
tailor

READING 16.2

In addition to the lifeguard position, Thanh found some other advertisements for work.

Classified Ads

(1)

HELP WANTED

HOTEL needs front desk clerk. **Night Shift** 11 p.m. - 6 a.m. Fri - Sun only. Experience reqd. Call **359-3987**.

(2)

Looking for **HOUSEKEEPERS** at large hotel. Must be neat. No exp. nec. **P/T or F/T** Fill out applic. at **Personnel Dept.:** *Hall's Hotel, 304 West St., New York, NY.*

(3)

CASHIERS wanted. English and Spanish fluency a must. No exp. nec. Hours flexible. Call **Ms. James, 225-3090** betw. 8 a.m. and 11 a.m. only.

(4)

P/T TEACHER'S AIDE

at recreation center. Exp. w/ children reqd. Ability to coach tennis or basketball a plus. Send resume to: **Carol Carter**, Director, *Fifth Ave. Recreation Center, 222 Fifth Ave, New York, N.Y. 10001.* **No phone calls.**

(5)

ASSEMBLY LINE WORKERS NEEDED. Top pay. 3 shifts avail.: Day, Eve., Night. Prefer F/T workers but P/T is avail. *Call 757-8075.* **No exp. nec.**

(6)

RECEPTIONIST

for busy office. Neat appearance a must. Pleasant personality. 2 yrs. minimum exp. 8-6 p.m. M-Th. **Call 553-9933.**

(7)

HOSPITAL STAFF

needed: receptionists, secretaries, nurse's aides, housekeepers. **P/T and F/T** *W/ or W/O exp.* Applic. accepted at **St. Mary's Hospital**, Personnel Dept. **M-F, 9-5.**

(8)

SALESPEOPLE NEEDED

for clothing store. No exp. necessary. **P/T or F/T** Bilingual preferred. Exp. helpful but not nec. Call 666-9345.

FOR SALE

ABBREVIATIONS IN WANT ADS

applic.:	application	**Days of the Week:**	M Monday
avail.:	available		Tu Tuesday
betw.:	between		W Wednesday
Dept.:	department		Th Thursday
exp.:	experience		F Friday
F/T:	full time		Sa Saturday
nec.:	necessary		Su Sunday
P/T:	part time		
reqd.:	required		
W/:	with		
W/O:	without		

UNDERSTANDING

1. **Look at the pictures below. Write the number of the want ad that matches the picture.**

  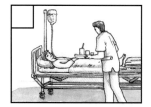 

2. **Check the correct box or boxes.**

	#1	#2	#3	#4	#5	#6	#7	#8
a. Which jobs require experience?								
b. Which job requires bilingual ability?								
c. Which want ads advertise more than one position?								

3. **Write *T* if the statement is true. Write *F* if the statement is false.**

   _____ **a.** If you want the cashier job in ad #3, you must work from 8 a.m. to 11 a.m.
   _____ **b.** If you want the teacher's aide job in ad #4, you must be able to coach tennis or basketball.
   _____ **c.** If you want the housekeeper job in ad #2, you must send a resume to the hotel.
   _____ **d.** The receptionist position in ad #6 is for a four-day-a-week job.

TALK ABOUT IT

Do you remember what Thanh said about herself and her job preferences? Reread her words below.

"I want a part time job that helps people. I don't care about just making money. I want to feel that my job does something good for people. My teachers say that I work very well with others. That's important to me. After school, I tutor some younger children in math. I'm also good at sports. I've thought about being a doctor or nurse but I can't stand the sight of blood!!"

Work in groups of three. Look at the job ads on page 106. Find two jobs that you think might be good for Thanh. Find two jobs which you think would be bad for Thanh. Talk about your reasons.

BEFORE READING 16.3

The following article is from the <u>Reader's Digest</u>. Don't try to understand every word as you read; just try to read the article to get the general ideas. In this article, 2 successful people talk about their first jobs. Before reading the article, interview 2 successful people you know. Ask them about their first jobs.

READING 16.3

My First Job

The Floor Mopper

"Be proud of what you do," my father always told me, "whether you're boss or mopping floors."

When I was 17, I got a summer job at Waterbury Hospital Health Center in Waterbury, Connecticut (U.S.A.), where I was told my duties would include–mopping floors. I smiled and remembered my Dad's advice.

Even though my job was the lowest, I was thrilled to have any work at all. Each morning, I imagined all the sick people not being able to eat if I wasn't there to scrub the pots. Once breakfast was done, I cleaned toilets, and in the late afternoon, mopped floors. Though I was dead tired, I wanted people to say, "That young man sure does a nice job."

Through every job I've ever held, my father's wise words have stayed with me. I've mopped floors, and I've been the boss. I think Dad would be proud.

Gary A. Franks is a political leader in the state of Connecticut in the northeastern U.S. Before that job, he was a successful real estate businessman.

The Assembly Line Worker

In 1949, when I was 13, my family managed to escape China, and a year later, we made our way to New York City. My first years in America were spent learning English and trying to get by in school. But by my senior year, I was near the top of the class.

Still, I was nervous as I looked for work that summer. I had never interviewed for a job. But my father was out of work, and I had to help support the family. I looked through the want ads every morning and called to arrange appointments. Finally, I found a job on the assembly line at the Swingline, Inc. stapler factory in Long Island City (in New York City). Placing little red tops on tiny staplers was boring, but it was great to be earning $40 a week.

The most important job I ever held was my first. Working on an assembly line for the minimum wage may not have been glamorous, but it gave me independence and allowed me to help my family.

John J. Sie is chairman and CEO of Encore Media Corp., a cable TV channel.

VOCABULARY

He's mopping floors.

She's scrubbing pots.

He's an assembly line worker.

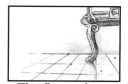

The floors shine.

proud	adj.	having and showing respect for or pleasure in one's self or another
thrilled	adj.	very excited
dead tired	adj.	really tired; exhausted
wise	adj.	showing intelligence and good sense (learned from experience)
to escape	v.	to get out from; to run away from
to get by	v.	to be good enough to pass but not very good
senior year	n.	the last year of high school or college
to be out of work	v.	to want a job but not have one
to support the family	v.	to provide the money for a family to live
minimum wage	n.	the lowest amount of money that a job can pay by law
glamorous	adj.	attractive and exciting
CEO	n.	chief executive officer; the top boss of a large company

1. Look at the pictures below.

Which pictures show work that Gary A. Franks did? Pictures #_____, _____, and _____.
Which picture shows work that John J. Sie did? Picture #_____.

2. Write *T* if the sentence is true. Write *F* if the sentence is false and correct it.

_____ **a.** Gary A. Franks' father told him that he should always be the boss.
_____ **b.** John J. Sie and his father worked at the stapler factory together.
_____ **c.** John J. Sie always passed his classes but he never did well.
_____ **d.** John J. Sie was born in the U.S.
_____ **e.** Gary A. Franks hated his first job.
_____ **f.** John J. Sie thought his first job was exciting.
_____ **g.** Gary A. Franks didn't think his first job was important.
_____ **h.** John J. Sie didn't think his first job was important.

LOOKING AT LANGUAGE

1. "Once" has many meanings. Look at the dictionary definition.

> **once** /wuns/ **1.** *adv.* one time and no more. *I visit her once a week.* **2.** *adv.* some time ago. *I could play tennis once but I can't anymore.* **3.** *conj.* from the moment that; when. *Once I heard his voice, I could not forget him.*

In Gary Frank's story, he says, "Once breakfast was done, I cleaned toilets." In this case, "once" means "when" (definition number 3 above). Look at the sentences below and write the number of the definition that fits the word *once*.

a. Once I was rich, but now I'm poor.   Definition #_____
b. Once he decides to do something, he always does it.   Definition #_____
c. I will only call her once.   Definition #_____

2. Gary A. Franks' father said "Be proud of what you do whether you're boss or mopping floors." "Whether" shows that there are two choices and something will happen in either case. Franks' father thinks he should be proud in either case. He should be proud if he's a boss. He should be proud if he's mopping floors. Look at the following sentences and answer the questions.

I will take the job whether it's part-time or full-time.
Will I take the job if it's part-time? _____ Will I take the job if it's full-time? _____

3. Look at the word that is circled. What is its reference? Draw an arrow to the word or words.

 a. Gary A. Franks is a political leader in the state of Connecticut in the northeastern U.S. Before that job, (he) was a successful real estate businessman.
 b. Working on an assembly line for the minimum wage may not have been glamorous but (it) gave me independence.

CHALLENGE

How much do you know about famous people and their work? Divide your class into teams (with 4 or 5 students per team). See how many your team can answer correctly. If you don't know, guess. After 10 minutes, see which team got the highest score.

1. Yousef Karsh (Turkey), André Kertész (Hungary), Henri Cartier Bresson (France) were all
   _____ a. architects   _____ b. political leaders   _____ c. photographers

2. Diego Rivera (Mexico), Paul Klee (Switzerland), and Georgia O'Keefe (U.S.) were all
   _____ a. political leaders   _____ b. photographers   _____ c. painters

3. Sir Christopher Wren (England), Antonio Gaudi (Spain), and Oscar Niemeyer (Brazil) were all
   _____ a. political leaders   _____ b. architects   _____ c. scientists

4. Giorgio Armani (Italy), Caroline Herrera (Venezuela) and Issey Miyake (Japan) are all
   _____ a. writers   _____ b. scientists   _____ c. fashion designers

5. Mikhail Baryshnikov (Latvia), Alicia Alonso (Cuba), and Lyn Seymour (Canada) were all
   _____ a. dancers   _____ b. fashion designers _____ c. writers

6. Dietrich Fischer-Dieskau (Germany), Dame Kiri Te Kanawa (New Zealand) and Dame Joan Sutherland (Australia) are all
   _____ a. dancers   _____ b. opera singers   _____ c. political leaders

7. Andrzej Wajda (Poland), Satyajit Ray (India) and Zhang Yimou (China, P.R.C.) are all
   _____ a. film actors   _____ b. film directors   _____ c. opera singers

8. Gabriel Garcia Marquez (Columbia), Naguib Mahfouz (Egypt), and Wole Soyinka (Nigeria) are all
   _____ a. dancers   _____ b. writers   _____ c. painters

9. Jana Novotna (Czech Republic), Amanda Coetzer (South Africa) and Stefan Edberg (Sweden) are all
   _____ a. film actors   _____ b. athletes   _____ c. writers

10. Lee Kuan Yew (Singapore), Lee Huan (Taiwan), Mohammad Najibullah (Afghanistan) were all
    _____ a. scientists   _____ b. political leaders   _____ c. athletes

QUOTES AND SAYINGS ABOUT WORK	• *A bad workman blames his tools.* • *Play is the work of a child.*

Graphology is the study of handwriting. Graphologists believe that you can understand a person's personality by looking at his or her handwriting. See if you can match the statements on the left with the statements on the right.

1. If a person's signature is much larger than his or her normal handwriting,

2. If a person's signature is much smaller than his or her normal handwriting,

3. If you can't read a person's family name in his or her signature,

4. If the handwriting obviously slants to the left,

5. If the handwriting obviously slants to the right,

6. If the slant of the handwriting jumps from left to right,

_____ a. the writer has feelings of anger or stress in relation to his or her family.

_____ b. the writer may be unstable or the writer may be lying or the writer may be feeling great stress.

_____ c. the writer wants attention.

_____ d. the writer is very emotional.

_____ e. the writer is modest (perhaps too modest) or wants to appear modest.

_____ f. the writer is probably holding back his or her true feelings.

Write a three-sentence letter to a person far away.

_____
_____
_____
_____

Sign your name: _____

Look at a classmate's paper. Can you understand anything about your classmate's personality by looking at his or her handwriting?

111

READING 17.1

The Herald

Survey: Who do you keep in touch with regularly?
How do you keep in touch?

Millie Lee
Engineer

Enrique Gomez
Student

Steve Lang
Auto Mechanic

Velia Morena
Lawyer

Surasaki Yawai
Businessman

Ana Yelsky
Student

"I keep in touch with my children. Both of them are students abroad. I write each of them at least twice a week. My daughter is a better letter writer than my son. She writes me every week. My son says he prefers to talk on the phone. I call them every Saturday morning. I miss them a lot but I'm glad they're happy."

"I keep in touch with my girlfriend. She's in New York studying fashion design. Neither one of us likes to write so we call each other every night. We talk for hours. We think it is important to keep our relationship close...but my phone bills are huge!!!"

"My wife and I have two kids and we really enjoy our jobs and our friends and our town. The only problem is that we are far from the kids' grandparents. We know how much they miss seeing their grandchildren grow up. Since we can't visit every month, we make a videotape instead. We tape the whole family at home, at school, at work. Everyone says something special to "grandma" and "grandpa."

"I travel a lot for business reasons. It's important for me to keep in touch with my office in case something needs my attention. I have a portable phone and a beeper. That way, my secretary can always reach me. Sometimes, we send messages by fax. If I need to see some important papers, my secretary can fax them to me wherever I am staying. Most hotels nowadays have a fax machine. Oh, excuse me. I think that's my beeper..."

"I keep in touch with my stockbroker. I invested a lot of money in the stock market. I need to know if the market is going up or down. I need to be ready to make a quick decision to buy or sell. I call every morning after I read the newspaper."

"I keep in touch with my childhood friends. Many of my friends are still in Moscow and I miss them. We keep in touch mostly by writing. The telephone is too expensive and often the connections aren't good. We sometimes send each other cassettes. When I play a cassette that my friend sent, I close my eyes and pretend she's sitting next to me. It makes me a little homesick but also happy."

YOUR TURN

What about you? Who do you keep in touch with regularly? How do you keep in touch — by mail? by phone? by fax? by sending cassettes or videos? in another way?

UNDERSTANDING

1. Fill in the blanks below with information from the survey on page 112.

   a. Millie keeps in touch with _____ by _____ and _____ .

   b. Enrique keeps in touch with _____ by _____ .

   c. Velia keeps in touch with _____ by _____ and _____ .

   d. Surasaki keeps in touch with _____ by _____ .

2. Write *T* if the sentence is true. Write *F* if the sentence is false.

   _____ **a.** Millie has two children.

   _____ **b.** Millie's children live near her.

   _____ **c.** Millie calls her children twice a week.

   _____ **d.** Enrique and his girlfriend like to write.

   _____ **e.** Enrique and his girlfriend speak to each other once a day.

   _____ **f.** Steve and his family make videotapes for the kids' grandparents.

   _____ **g.** Ana mostly writes letters to her friends and sometimes sends cassettes.

VOCABULARY PRACTICE: OFFICE EQUIPMENT

phone	portable phone	fax	computer
typewriter	answering machine	calculator	copier

Fill in the blanks below with a kind of office equipment.

1. If I want to send a letter immediately from New York to Japan, I can send the letter by _____. I put a copy of the letter in the machine in my office and in seconds, people in Japan receive a copy of my letter.

2. A secretary needs to type a letter. He can use a _____ or a _____ .

3. A businessman is expecting an important call but he has to leave his office. He can carry a _____ .

4. A businesswoman phoned but no one was in the office. She left a message on the _____ .

5. How much is 57,815,075 ÷ 28.3? If you want a quick answer, use a

READING 17.2

When you use a public telephone, what do you do? Do you use a telephone card? Do you need a special token? Do you use coins? Do you use a credit card? The instructions below tell how to use a public telephone in the United States.

COIN DEPOSIT CALLS
     LOCAL AND WITHIN AREA CODE....................... Dial Phone Number
     LONG DISTANCE (Outside of area codes)........... Dial 1 + Area Code + Phone Number

OPERATOR ASSISTED CALLS (COLLECT AND PERSON TO PERSON)
     LOCAL.. Dial 0 + Area Code + Phone Number
     LONG DISTANCE... Dial 0 + Area Code + Phone Number

DIRECTORY ASSISTANCE
     LOCAL.. Dial 411
     LONG DISTANCE... Dial 1 + Area Code + 555-1212

REPAIRS AND REFUNDS... Dial 611

EMERGENCY... Dial 911

VOCABULARY PRACTICE: PHONE CALLS

When you want to make a phone call, you pick up the <u>receiver</u>. When you hear <u>the dial tone</u>, you can <u>dial</u> your call. If the call is in the same area, it is <u>a local call</u>. If your call is <u>long distance</u>, you need to dial <u>an area code</u> before dialing the phone number.

If you do not have money, you can <u>call collect</u>. Before you can speak, <u>an operator</u> will ask the person who picks up the phone, "Do you accept the charges?" If the person answers "yes," this means he or she will pay for the phone call.

If you are calling long-distance and you only want to speak to one person, you can call <u>person-to-person.</u>   If somebody else answers the phone, you don't have to pay for the call.

If you do not know someone's number, you can call <u>directory assistance</u>. You can give the operator the name and address of the person you want to call. She or he will help you find the number.

If you <u>deposit</u> money, but you can't make your call, <u>hang up</u>. If you don't get your money back, press the <u>coin release lever</u>. If that doesn't work, call the phone company to get a <u>refund</u>.

SCANNING

How fast can you answer the questions below, using the information on page 114? Write *T* if the sentence is true. Write *F* if the sentence is false.

_____   1. If you lose money in a phone machine, you can call 911 for a refund.

_____   2. If you want to call your neighbor but you don't know her number, you can dial 1 + Area Code + 555-1212 for help.

_____   3. If you want to make a local call, you can deposit coins and dial the phone number.

_____   4. If you want to report a broken phone, you call 411.

_____   5. If you want to make a collect local call, you dial 0 + the phone number.

_____   6. If there's a fire and you want to call the fire department, call 911.

_____   7. Dial "1" before all long distance calls.

_____   8. If you need help finding someone's phone number, call directory assistance.

_____   9. If you want to call long distance collect, dial 1 + Area Code + Phone Number.

_____ 10. For long distance directory assistance, dial 411.

TALK ABOUT IT

When are the cheapest times to make long distance phone calls?

When are the most expensive times to make long distance phone calls?

What are the disadvantages of calling collect and calling person-to-person?

Can you call another country without operator assistance? How?

BEFORE READING 17.3

The reading below is about handwriting. Some people believe that your handwriting shows a lot about your personality. Before reading the article, show your classmate a page of your normal handwriting. Is it neat or messy? Are your letters large or small? Do you think your handwriting says something about your personality? Look at the title of the reading: Your "I" Says A Lot. What do you think this reading is about?

READING 17.3

Your "I" Says A Lot

Your "I" says a lot. According to Malcolm Ater, a graphologist, it's probably the most important clue into the writer's personality and opinion of himself or herself. If you look at the way writers dot their "i's", he says, you can learn a lot about them.

Dots placed very high show curiosity and ambition.

Dots that are placed low show calmness and care.

Dots placed to the left of the "i" show procrastination.

Dots placed to the right of the "i" show impatience.

Dots placed directly above the "i," (either high or low), show care.

Dots that are very heavy show willpower.

Dots that are very light show caution and low energy.

Dots that are missing show carelessness and impatience.

Dots that are short lines show excitability.

Dots that are wavy lines show friendliness.

Dots that are circled show creativity.

Take a look at your own writing. What do your "i's" say about you?

VOCABULARY

clue	n.	something that helps to find an answer to a question
curiosity	n.	the characteristic of loving to learn or know
ambition	n.	the characteristic of wanting success and power
calmness	n.	the characteristic of being calm or peaceful
care	n.	the characteristic of paying attention to details
impatience	n.	the characteristic of not being able to wait calmly; without patience
procrastination	n.	the characteristic of not taking care of things right away (and waiting to take care of them later)
carelessness	n.	the characteristic of not being careful, not paying attention to small things
willpower	n.	the strength of mind to make something happen
caution	n.	the characteristic of paying attention to avoid danger
excitability	n.	the characteristic of getting excited easily
creativity	n.	the characteristic of making things or thinking in new and different ways

UNDERSTANDING

Use the information from page 116 to answer the questions below.

1. Michael Jones wants to be famous and rich. Which "i" is probably his?

    _____ a. *i*   _____ b. *i*   _____ c. *i*

2. Leola Tabor is an artist. Which "i" is probably hers?

    _____ a. *i*   _____ b. *i*   _____ c. *i*

3. Maria Soto hates waiting for people and things. Which "i" is probably hers?

    _____ a. *i*   _____ b. *i*   _____ c. *i*

4. When you ask Kim to do something, he always says "Tomorrow." Which "i" is probably his?

    _____ a. *i*   _____ b. *i*   _____ c. *i*

5. Which person would probably be good to hire to build a house?

    _____ a. *i*   _____ b. *i*   _____ c. *i*

LOOKING AT LANGUAGE

1. *Calm* is an adjective. *Calmness* is a noun. **Find two other words in the reading that end with *-ness*.**

    _____ and _____

2. *Curious* is an adjective. *Curiosity* is a noun. **Find two other words in the reading that end with *-ity*.**

    _____ and _____

3. *Care* means "the characteristic of paying attention to details." *Careless* describes someone without that characteristic. **Check the words below where *-less* means without.**

    _____ friendless   _____ jobless   _____ lesson

4. *Care* means "the characteristic of paying attention to details". *Careful* describes someone who is full of that characteristic. **Check the words below where *-ful* means full of.**

    _____ beautiful   _____ harmful   _____ thoughtful

5. **Look at the word that is circled. What is its reference? Draw an arrow to the word or words.**

    a. Your "I" says a lot. According to Malcom Ater, a graphologist, (it's) probably the most important clue into the writer's personality.
    b. If you look at the way writers dot their *i*'s, you can learn a lot about (them).

CHALLENGE

Who invented the telephone? Fill in the blanks with words from Unit 17. When you finish, read the circled letters.

1.

2. This is a person's name written at the end of a letter or on a check.

3. This machine can send a copy of a letter to another country in minutes.

4. This is the way someone writes.

5.

6. You can leave a _____ on an answering machine.

7. If you need help when making a phone call, talk to an _____.

8. The opposite of light is _____.

9. Someone who wants power and success has this characteristic.

10. The opposite of careful is _____.

11. A phone call to someone in your neighborhood is not a long distance call. It is a _____ call.

QUOTES AND SAYINGS ABOUT COMMUNICATING	• *Silence is golden.* • *Actions speak louder than words.*

Look at the picture of an auto repair shop below. Many things in this picture are unsafe. Make a list of the safety problems you see.

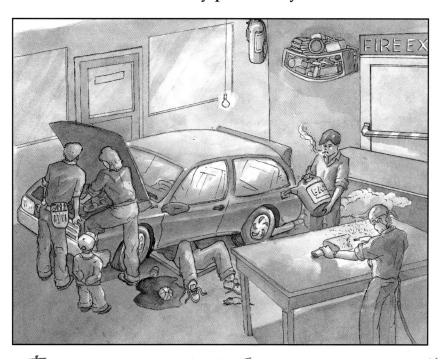

Example: _There is not enough light. The workers can't see well._

_____
_____
_____
_____
_____
_____

What could happen in this shop because of the safety problems?

_____
_____
_____

What should the owner do to make the shop safer?

_____
_____
_____

READING 18.1

Linda, Steve, and Rae work together. It's Tuesday morning and Steve is late. Read the conversation.

Linda: It's 9:30. Isn't Steve usually here by now?
Rae: Usually. He's rarely late. I hope nothing is wrong.

(Steve walks in, limping, with a bandaged hand.)

Linda: Steve! What happened to you?
Steve: What didn't happen to me? Everything happened to me. I sprained my ankle, burned my hand, cut my finger. What else? Oh, yes. I lost my wallet, too.
Rae: How? Where?
Steve: Well, it all started when I left work yesterday. My car was in the repair shop so I had to take the bus. You know my bus doesn't run often so when I saw the bus coming, I ran to get to the bus stop.
Rae: And?
Steve: I didn't know my shoelace was untied.
Rae: Oh, no.
Steve: Oh yes. I tripped on my shoelace. Luckily, I wasn't too badly hurt — just a sprained ankle — so I got up and limped to the bus.
Linda: That's too bad.
Steve: That wasn't all. When I got home, I realized that I didn't have my wallet. I think it fell out of my pocket when I tripped. What a pain! I lost my money, my credit cards, my driver's license...
Linda: That *is* a pain.
Steve: Then, I decided to relax and make dinner. That was a mistake!! I cut myself while chopping carrots and then I spilled hot tea on my hand. After that, I just decided not to do anything at all. I just went to bed.
Rae: Why don't you sit down and relax for a few minutes? Work can wait.
Steve: Thanks. I think I will.
Linda: Wait. Don't. That chair is...

(Steve begins to sit down)

Linda: ....broken.

UNDERSTANDING

1. **Where did Steve sprain his ankle? Check the correct answer.**

    _____ on the street   _____ on the bus   _____ in the office   _____ in his house

2. **Where did Steve probably lose his wallet? Check the correct answer.**

    _____ on the street   _____ on the bus   _____ in the office   _____ in his house

3. **Where did Steve cut himself? Check the correct answer.**

    _____ on the street   _____ on the bus   _____ in the office   _____ in his house

4. **How did Steve burn himself? Check the correct picture.**

5. **Why did Steve trip? Check the correct picture.**

6. **Write *T* if the sentence is true. Write *F* if the sentence is false. Write *?* if you don't know from the story.**

    _____ **a.** Steve is often late to work.

    _____ **b.** Steve always takes the bus to work.

    _____ **c.** Steve's bus runs frequently.

    _____ **d.** Steve broke his leg.

    _____ **e.** Linda knew the office chair was broken before Steve sat in it.

    _____ **f.** Rae knew the office chair was broken before Steve sat in it.

VOCABULARY PRACTICE: PARTS OF THE BODY

Work with a partner. Look at the words in the box. Put these words into the categories given below.

Parts of the Head	Parts of the Arm	Parts of the Leg
_____	_____	_____
_____	_____	_____
_____	_____	_____
_____	_____	_____
_____	_____	_____
_____		

forehead   eyelid
tongue   thigh
ear   wrist
fingernail   heel
chin   knee
elbow   calf
thumb   knuckle
toe   jaw

DO IT

Work in groups of three to act out the dialogue on page 120.

121

READING 18.2

If someone is hurt, do you know what to do? Read about emergency medical aid for three medical problems.

If Someone Has a Nose Bleed...

1. Using your fingers, squeeze just under the bridge of the nose.
2. Tilt the head back if bleeding is not severe.
3. Keep the patient quiet.
4. Apply ice around the patient's nose.
5. Place cotton deep into the patient's nose.

   If bleeding can't be stopped, call for medical aid.

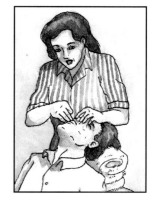

If Someone Faints...

1. Place the patient on his back with his head lower than his feet.
2. Loosen the patient's clothing and keep the patient warm.
3. Do not give the patient any liquids or food.
4. Have the patient rest for at least 15 minutes.

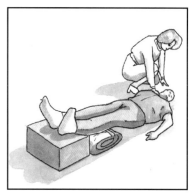

If Someone Gets a Scorpion Sting...

1. Place the patient on her back.
2. Keep the patient calm. Do not allow the patient to walk or move, if unnecessary.
3. Cover the patient with a blanket.
4. Apply ice to the area of the sting.
5. Call for medical help or take the patient to a doctor immediately.

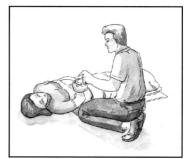

VOCABULARY

emergency	*n.*	a problem needing immediate attention
aid	*n.*	help
to apply	*v.*	to put on (medicine, for example)
sting	*n.*	a bite from an insect (such as a bee)
calm	*adj.*	not excited; relaxed
to allow	*v.*	to give permission; to let someone do something
unnecessary	*adj.*	not needed or required

loose tie

tight tie

UNDERSTANDING

1. **Work with a partner to practice giving and following the directions below.**
   a. Squeeze just under the bridge of your nose.
   b. Squeeze your nose.
   c. Squeeze your wrist.
   d. Tilt your head to the right.
   e. Tilt your head back.
   f. Tilt your head to the left.

2. **Draw a line to match the sentence with the picture.**

   a. The patient is on his back with his head lower than his feet.

   b. The patient is covered with a blanket.

   c. Someone is applying ice to the area of the sting.

3. **Write *T* if the sentence is true, according to the reading on page 122. Write *F* if the sentence is false.**

   _____ a. You can help a person who fainted by giving him something cold to drink.

   _____ b. It is important to get medical aid for a person with a scorpion sting.

   _____ c. Ice is useful for a nose bleed and a scorpion sting.

   _____ d. You should always call for medical aid when a person has a nose bleed.

   _____ e. You should always tilt the patient's head back if he has a nose bleed.

   _____ f. A patient should lie down if she has a scorpion sting.

TALK ABOUT IT

1. Have you ever needed emergency medical aid? What happened?
2. Have you ever given someone emergency medical aid? What happened?

BEFORE READING 18.3

"Motion sickness" is a sick feeling that some people get when they travel by car, bus, boat, or train. Do you ever get "motion sickness"? When? What do you do about it?

READING 18.3

MOTION SICKNESS: TIPS FOR THE TRAVELER

1 Imagine this. You're on your way to the mountains. You've got your bus ticket. You're ready for the trip. The first part of the trip goes well. You leave the city. The scenery begins to change. But then the road starts getting more narrow...and curvier. You start to sweat. Perhaps you get a headache. You feel nauseated. You want to get off the bus.

2 What happened? You experienced motion sickness — a fairly common feeling among people who travel by car, bus, boat, or train. It happens because the movement (of the car, bus, boat, or train) is affecting your sense of balance in your inner ear.

3 Here are some tips for the traveler. Keep them in mind and make your travels more pleasant.

PREVENTION

- **Sea Travel**

4 Try to stay outside on the deck, where you can see the horizon.
Avoid heavy meals while traveling, though a light snack might help.
Lie down if there is room.
Don't read or play games that require focusing on moving objects or words.
Stay in the midline of the boat. This part moves less than the sides.
Take motion sickness medicine 30 minutes to 1 hour prior to traveling.

- **Road/Train Travel**

5 Try to travel in the front seat.
Focus on the road ahead.
Do not eat or drink just before traveling.
Try not to sit near smokers.
Sit still.
Do not read or play games that require focusing on moving objects or words or stationary objects inside the car.
Take motion sickness medicine 30 minutes to 1 hour prior to traveling.

TREATMENT

6
- Put a few drops of peppermint oil on a handkerchief, and smell it if you feel nauseated.
- Chew a piece of fresh, peeled ginger root.
- Place your right thumb on the inside of your left wrist. Massage with the thumb, using a deep circular motion, for one minute while taking deep breaths. Then do the same on the other side.

VOCABULARY

a narrow and curvy road

he is sweating

she feels nauseated

deck   horizon

ginger root

tip	*n.*	piece of advice
a sense of balance	*n.*	a feeling that all parts are equal or fitting together well
to keep in mind	*v.*	to remember
pleasant	*adj.*	enjoyable
to prevent	*v.*	to not allow something to happen
to focus	*v.*	to put all of one's attention somewhere
still; stationary	*adj.*	unmoving

AFTER READING 18.3

1. **Look at these pictures. Which pictures show people doing the right thing to prevent motion sickness? Check them.**

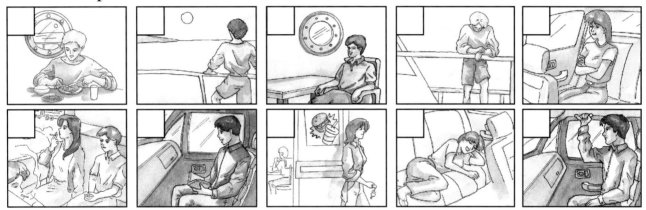

2. **One treatment for motion sickness is a kind of massage. Demonstrate that massage.**

LOOKING AT LANGUAGE

1. **Match the words with their opposites.**

   _____ keep in mind   **a.** stand up
   _____ prior to   **b.** a snack
   _____ lie down   **c.** curvy
   _____ straight   **d.** forget
   _____ a heavy meal   **e.** stationary; still
   _____ moving   **f.** after

2. **Look at the word that is circled. What is its reference? Draw an arrow to the word or words.**

   a. Imagine (this.) You're on your way to the mountains. You've got your bus ticket. You're ready for the trip. The first part of the trip goes well. You leave the city. But then the road starts getting more narrow and curvier. You feel nauseated. You want to get off the bus.

   b. Here are some tips for the traveler. Keep (them) in mind.

   c. Stay in the midline of the boat. (This part) moves less than the sides.

CHALLENGE

Omar had a terrible day yesterday. He lost his wallet, sprained his ankle, had a nose bleed and stained his shirt with blood, left his keys in his car and locked the doors, fought with his boss, burned his hand and received a traffic ticket. What a day!!

Read the clues below and see if you can figure out what happened first, second, third, and so on.

Clues
(**Note:** All the clues talk about the same day and are not in the correct order.)

Clue A: When the policeman stopped him to give him a speeding ticket, Omar was on his way to the dry cleaners. The policeman wondered about the blood on his shirt.

Clue B: Omar didn't drive to work because his car was in the repair shop. He was glad he didn't have to drive because his right hand still hurt from the spilled coffee.

Clue C: Omar locked his keys in the car so he couldn't get into the house. For ten minutes, he sat on the steps and waited for his wife to come home from her office. He tried to rest his aching ankle. She didn't return.

Clue D: Omar picked up his car from the auto repair shop and paid his bill at 4:45. He was careful in the shop because he didn't want his clean white shirt to get dirty.

Clue E: While running for the bus to get to work, Omar tripped on his shoelaces and sprained his ankle. He was hurt but his clothes were fine.

Clue F: Omar always keeps his driver's license, all of his credit cards, his telephone calling card, and his money in his wallet.

Clue G: The auto repair shop closes at 5:00 so Omar left work early to get his car on the way home.

Clue H: Omar took off his bloody shirt and gave it to the dry cleaners when he brought in his order. He paid his bill with cash.

Clue I: Omar's boss got angry with him right before lunch because he couldn't find an important report.

Clue J: Omar walked to the corner grocery store. He deposited the coins and called his wife from a pay phone. She returned home and opened the door for him.

Put a *1* next to the first thing that happened, a *2* next to the second thing that happened, a *3* next to the third thing, and so on.

_____ He lost his wallet.

_____ He sprained his ankle.

_____ He had a nose bleed and stained his shirt with blood.

_____ He left all his keys (car, house, and office) in his car and locked the doors.

_____ He fought with his boss.

_1_ He burned his hand.

_____ He got a traffic ticket.

_____ He took a bus.

_____ He couldn't get into his house because he didn't have his keys.

_____ He got his car from the repair shop.

_____ He went into the dry cleaners.

Our world is faced with many problems. What, in your opinion, are the three biggest problems facing our world today? The pictures below may give you some ideas but you may think of others.

Air and water pollution

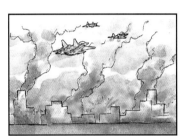

Wars

Guns

Hunger

Nuclear power

Violence on TV

Poverty

Overpopulation

Discrimination

Destruction of the land

Disease

Illiteracy

Crime

Talk to a classmate and ask these questions:

What, in your opinion, are the most important problems facing our world?

What, in your opinion, are the most important problems facing your home country?

What, in your opinion, are the most important problems facing your neighborhood?

READING 19.1

The Herald

Wednesday, April

Survey: In your opinion, what is an important problem facing the world today? What can we do about it?

Michelle Ryder School Counselor	**Arturo Velez** Photographer	**Lou Shelton** Teacher	**Carl Johnson** Doctor	**Mai Nguyen** Homemaker	**Bev Cassey** Reporter

"To me, overpopulation is a real problem. Our earth cannot feed the growing number of people. In 1800, the world population was less than 1 billion. In 1900, it was less than 2 billion. In 1960, it was just about 3 billion. In 1975, it was more than 4 billion. Now, it is more than 5 billion people. Our population is increasing too fast. Can the Earth take care of so many people? I think the only solution is to have fewer children."

"I worry about the environment. We are destroying our air, our water, our forests. We produce so much garbage and pollution. One thing that we can do is recycle. We can reuse glass, paper, cans and even plastics."

"I think poverty is a very serious problem. Our world is divided into "haves" and "have-nots." I don't think it is right that some people have beautiful houses, cars, clothes, while other people don't even have food or a place to live. I think we need to think about the world as "us" not "us and them". I believe that we need to share the wealth of the world more."

"I think the biggest problem is war. People fight about religion, about land, about power. This is not new but fighting is different now because we have so many new and dangerous weapons. Nuclear power can destroy us all. I think the answer is in cooperation. People need to work together for everyone's good. I think organizations like the United Nations have problems but they are very important."

"I worry about health problems. A disease like AIDS, for example, can destroy us all. I think we need to spend a lot more money on scientific research to find cures for diseases and work together to improve the health of people all over the world. There is an organization called "Doctors Without Borders". They are doctors and nurses from all over the world who travel to poor countries to help the sick. I really respect that group."

"I worry about the world's children. Some are homeless. Some are illiterate. Some are using drugs. They see violence on TV and in their world. What are they learning? Who is taking care of them? I think we must pay attention to the needs of the children."

UNDERSTANDING

1. Match the picture with the person who talked about that problem.

Michelle

Arturo

Lou

Carl

Mai

Bev

2. Look at this button. Who would probably wear it?

_____ Michelle and Arturo   _____ Carl and Arturo   _____ Mai and Carl

3. Look at this button. Who would probably wear it?

_____ Carl and Arturo   _____ Mai and Michelle   _____ Mai and Carl

4. What solutions did each person suggest?

   a. Michelle believes that one way to solve the problem of overpopulation is
   _____.

   b. Arturo believes that one way to solve the problem of environmental destruction is
   _____.

   c. Carl believes that one way to solve the problem of war is _____.

   d. Mai believes that two ways to solve health problems are _____
      and _____.

THINK ABOUT IT

What do you think this button means? Which of the people on page 128 would probably wear it?

VOCABULARY PRACTICE: OUR ENVIRONMENT

Look at these three drawings. Work with a partner. How many objects can you label?

tree

READING 19.2

Michelle Ryder, on p.128, feels that "overpopulation is a real problem." Look at the following charts giving information about population. Do you agree with Ms. Ryder?

Growth of World Population by Billions and Year (Past and Projected)

World Population	Year
1 billion	1805
2 billion	1926
3 billion	1960
4 billion	1974
5 billion	1987
6 billion	1998
7 billion	2010
8 billion	2023

Projected Population Growth by Geographic Region 1985-2025

Region	Population (millions)		Growth Rate (%)		Birth Rate (per 1,000)		Death Rate (per 1,000)	
	1985	2025	1985-90	2020-5	1985-90	2020-5	1985-90	2020-5
World	4840	8188	1.71	0.94	26.9	17.6	9.8	8.2
Africa	560	1495	3.05	1.74	45.0	24.1	14.5	6.7
Asia	2819	4758	1.80	0.89	27.4	17.0	9.2	8.1
Americas	666	1035	1.58	0.72	23.4	15.3	7.9	8.2
Europe	770	863	0.45	0.15	14.7	13.0	10.3	11.5
Oceania	25	36	1.37	0.59	19.6	15.0	8.2	9.1

VOCABULARY

1 billion = 1,000,000,000
1 million = 1,000,000
Projected population = expectations about the population in the future
Growth Rate = a number telling how fast (by what %) the population is growing
Birth Rate (per 1,000) = the number of births for every 1,000 people
Death Rate (per 1,000) = the number of deaths for every 1,000 people

UNDERSTANDING

Using the information in the charts on page 130, answer the following questions.

1. What is the projected world population for the year 2010? _____

2. What was the world population in 1985? _____

3. What was the population of Europe in 1985? _____

4. What is the projected population of Europe in the year 2025? _____

5. What was the growth rate in Africa between 1985 and 1990? _____

6. What was the birth rate in Asia between 1985 and 1990? _____

7. What is the projected birth rate in Asia between 2020 and 2025? _____

8. How long did it take the world to grow from 1 billion to 2 billion people? _____

9. How long did it take the world to grow from 2 billion to 3 billion people? _____

10. How long did it take the world to grow from 4 billion to 5 billion people? _____

11. What region grew the fastest between 1985 and 1990? _____

12. What region grew the slowest between 1985 and 1990? _____

13. What region had the lowest death rate between 1985 and 1990? _____

14. What region has the projected lowest death rate between 2020 and 2025? _____

15. In what year will the world population reach 7 billion? _____

Write *T* if the sentence is true. Write *F* if the sentence is false.

_____ 1. The projected world population for the year 2025 is less than 8 billion people.
_____ 2. The world population in 1985 was 4,840,000.
_____ 3. Oceania's population is growing faster than Asia's population.
_____ 4. Between 1985 and 1990, Africa had the highest birth rate and the highest death rate.
_____ 5. Between 2020 and 2025, Africa has the highest projected birth rate and the highest projected death rate.

THINK ABOUT IT

What does zero population growth mean?
Why is the population growing so quickly?

DO IT

Find out the population, birth rate, and death rate in your home country.

BEFORE READING 19.3

The title of this article, "Are You A Giraffe?" is unusual. What might this title mean? Think about the characteristics of giraffes. What kind of animal is a giraffe? In what ways might a person be like a giraffe?

READING 19.3

Are You A Giraffe?

1   Retirees Claude and Louise Montgomery are giraffes. So are police officers George Hankins and George Pearson. These men and women don't look like giraffes; they look like you and me. Then, why do people call them "giraffes"?

2   A giraffe, they say, is an animal that sticks its neck out, can see for miles, has a large heart, and leads a peaceful life with grace and dignity. A "giraffe" is a person who believes in the importance of "sticking his or her neck out" for others, has a vision of future possibilities, has compassion for others, and lives a peaceful and dignified life.

3   "The Giraffe Project" is a 10-year-old organization which finds and honors "giraffes" in the U.S. and worldwide. The organization's goal is to encourage individuals to do something to create a better world. The organization believes that a person shouldn't hide his or her head (like a turtle); instead, the organization tells people to "stick your neck out" and help others. Claude and Louise Montgomery, George Hankins, and George Pearson are only a few of the nearly, 1,000 "giraffes" that the organization has found and honored.

4   Claude and Louise Montgomery entered their retirement with some money that they saved for an emergency. One day, however, they saw a homeless man looking for a place to keep warm and they decided that *that* was their emergency. Today, they live in Friendship House, where they invite twelve homeless people to stay every night. Claude and Louise Montgomery are certainly "giraffes."

5   Police officers George Hankins and George Pearson work in a large city. They see crime every day and their work is sometimes dangerous. They work hard for their money. However, these two men put their savings together and even borrowed money to start a youth center in a violent and poor part of the city. George Hankins and George Pearson are certainly "giraffes."

6   Do you know anyone who is a "giraffe"? In what way? "The Giraffe Project" would like to hear about "giraffes" worldwide. Write to The Giraffe Project, P.O. Box 759, Langley, WA 98260, USA and tell them about the giraffes you know.

VOCABULARY

retiree	*n.*	a retired person
grace	*n.*	beauty of movement and behavior
dignity	*n.*	self-respect
vision	*n.*	ability to see; ability to understand the true meaning of things (especially, in the future)
compassion	*n.*	sympathy or understanding of the feelings and pain of others
dignified	*adj.*	describing something or someone having dignity
to honor	*v.*	to have respect for and show respect to (someone)
goal	*n.*	purpose; aim; something one wishes to reach or get
to encourage	*v.*	to give hope or confidence or support to (someone)
individual	*n.*	a single person or member of a group
to borrow	*v.*	to take something for a short period of time but plan to return it
violent	*adj.*	showing great and harmful physical force

If someone **sticks her neck out**, this means she does something more than people usually do or expect. Sticking one's neck out involves taking a chance; it may involve possible danger or possible loss.

UNDERSTANDING

1. **Draw a line and match the words on the right to the words on the left to make true sentences.**

Claude and Louise Montgomery	help young people in a poor neighborhood.
The Giraffe Project	is an animal with a long neck.
A giraffe	help people without homes.
George Hankins and George Pearson	is an organization that honors "giraffes".

2. **Write *T* if the sentence is true. Write *F* if the sentence is false.**

_____ **a.** The "Giraffe Project" is an organization that protects animals.

_____ **b.** The "Giraffe Project" is only interested in working with large companies and businesses.

_____ **c.** The "Giraffe Project" only works in the U.S.

_____ **d.** The "Giraffe Project" wants individuals to help others.

_____ **e.** The "Giraffe Project" only found 4 "giraffes" in the world.

LOOKING AT LANGUAGE

1. **Sometimes, when quotation marks are around words, it means that the writer is using the words in an unusual way. Look at this example from the reading.**

A "giraffe" is a person who believes in the importance of "sticking his or her neck out" for others.

A giraffe is usually an animal but in this case, a "giraffe" is a person. The expression "to stick your neck out" in this sentence, does not mean moving your neck.

Look at the following sentences. Talk with your classmates about what you think each sentence means.
a. My 3-year-old daughter "washed" my car.
b. Her "friend" never calls her.

2. **The reading says, "Retirees Claude and Louise Montgomery are giraffes. <u>So are police officers George Hankins and George Pearson</u>". What does this mean? Check your answer:**

_____ George Hankins and George Pearson are retired, just like the Montgomerys.

_____ George Hankins and George Pearson are giraffes, just like the Montgomerys.

_____ The Montgomerys are police officers, just like George Hankins and George Pearson.

3. **Look at the words that are circled. What are their references? Draw arrows to the word or words.**

Claude and Louise Montgomery entered (their) retirement with some money that (they) saved for an emergency. One day, however, (they) saw a homeless man looking for a place to keep warm and (they) decided that (that) was their emergency.

CHALLENGE

All of the words in the crossword puzzle are in Unit 19. Can you complete the puzzle?

Across Clues

2. The Pacific _____
3. The Nile _____
5. 1,000,000,000 equals a _____.
6. A _____ is an animal with a long neck.
7. When there is unclean water or air, we have air and water _____.
10. People without homes are _____ people.

Down Clues

1. 1,000,000 equals a _____.
2. The United Nations and The Giraffe Project are two _____.
4. The opposite of war is _____.
8. A _____ is a body of water with land all around it.
9. The opposite of rich is _____.

| QUOTES AND SAYINGS ABOUT CARING FOR OUR WORLD AND EACH OTHER | • *If you're not part of the solution, you're part of the problem.* • *Do unto others as you would have them do unto you.* |

There are many stories and poems about nature. Here are two. The first poem is by Gogisgi/Carroll Arnett, an American poet of Cherokee (a Native American tribe) and French descent. Gogisgi is his Cherokee name and means "smoke". He is the author of 10 collections of poetry. The second poem is by Carl Sandburg, an American poet of Swedish descent. He is the author of several books of poetry and non-fiction.

Early Song
by Gogisgi/Carroll Arnett

As the sun rises
high enough to
warm the frost
off the pine needles,

I rise to make
four prayers of
thanksgiving for
this fine clear day,

for this good brown
earth, for all
brothers and sisters,
for the dark blood

that runs through me
in a great circle
back into this
good brown earth.

pine tree

TALK ABOUT IT

1. What time of day is it in the poem? Why do you say this?
2. What time of year is it in the poem? Why do you say this?
3. Is the speaker in the poem alone or with someone? Why do you say this?
4. Why does the speaker say <u>four</u> prayers of thanksgiving?
5. From a Native American viewpoint, everything on the earth is connected — people, animals, nature. Does Arnett's poem express this viewpoint? How?
6. Is Arnett's view of nature a positive or a negative one? Why do you say this?

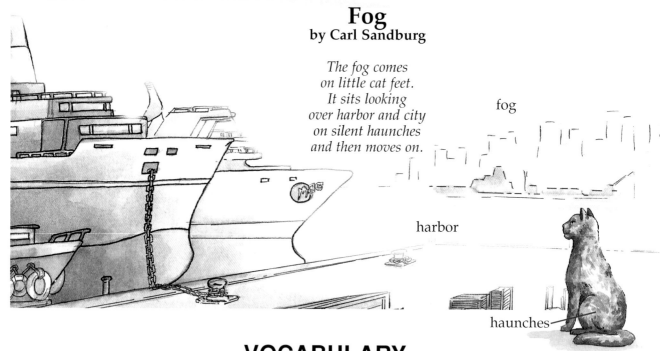

Fog
by Carl Sandburg

*The fog comes
on little cat feet.
It sits looking
over harbor and city
on silent haunches
and then moves on.*

fog

harbor

haunches

VOCABULARY

harbor   *n.*   an area of calm, deep, and protected water in which boats can be safe
silent   *adj.*   not making a sound

TALK ABOUT IT

Poets paint pictures with words. Sometimes, in order to describe something, they compare it to something completely different. Through that comparison, the poet hopes the reader will get a deeper sense of the object being described.

1. What does Sandburg want to describe?
2. What does he use as a comparison?
3. Imagine in your mind a cat moving as Sandburg describes it: "on little feet," "it sits looking...on silent haunches and then moves on." How can the fog be like this cat?
4. What feeling do you have as you read this? (Do you feel restless? Peaceful? Frightened? Something else?)

TRY IT

You want to describe a terrible storm. What animal could you compare it to? What color could you compare it to? What kind of musical instrument could you compare it to?

You want to describe a clear, spring day. What animal could you compare it to? What color could you compare it to? What kind of musical instrument could you compare it to?

John

Jessie

Christopher

Liza

Steve

Michelle

KEN

Stella

Siti

Unit 1

1. Susie, 4, wavy, blonde, green
2. Karen, 6, curly, light brown, brown
3. Lena, 11, wavy, blonde, brown
4. Jim, 12, curly, red, brown
5. Joe, 13, straight, light brown, brown

Unit 2

Across:

6. equipment   8. wear   9. shape
11. tennis   13. coach

Down:

1. court   2. rent   3. fee   4. athletic
5. sports   7. physical   8. win   10. lose
12. not

Unit 3

P	H	A	R	C	A	P	S	C	W	I	N	D
N	P	I	Z	Z	Y	H	A	O	H	O	M	E
C	U	H	E	A	D	A	C	H	E	L	E	N
O	O	R	Y	H	P	R	D	O	E	N	D	P
N	D	U	S	S	A	M	R	S	L	A	I	H
G	R	O	G	E	I	A	O	N	C	D	C	Y
E	T	H	S	H	N	C	W	O	H	I	I	S
S	R	E	M	E	D	Y	S	D	A	Z	N	I
T	D	F	A	I	Y	Z	Y	A	I	Z	E	C
I	P	R	E	G	N	A	N	T	R	Y	A	I
O	R	R	U	V	C	A	P	S	U	L	E	A
N	C	L	O	G	E	D	O	C	T	O	R	N
E	D	O	N	U	T	R	I	T	I	O	U	S

Unit 4

1. c   2. b   3. c   4. a   5. c
6. c   7. a   8. c   9. c   10. b

Unit 5

It was probably Jack. Liz Aaron says that she only takes
the ring off to bathe or wash the dishes. Liz Aaron
remembers putting the ring on before the party.

Unit 6

1. c   2. a   3. a   4. c   5. c
6. b   7. c   8. b   9. a   10. c

Unit 7

Across:

1. estimate   7. neighborhood   8. farm
11. re   12. repair   13. garage   15. closet

Down:

1. ex   2. tunnel   3. handyman   4. wilderness
5. prompt   6. rocking   9. architect
10. plumber   14. rate

Unit 8

Suha is going to the graduation party which begins
at 7:00.
Rita is going to the housewarming party which begins
at 7:30.
David is going to the birthday party which begins
at 8:00.
Lidia is going to the dinner party which begins at 8:30.
Paul is going to the wedding party which begins
at 9:00.

Unit 9

L	I	P	L	E	A	S	E	D	E	A	N	E	R
H	A	R	A	F	O	N	E	R	V	O	U	S	A
E	A	D	I	R	R	I	T	A	B	L	E	R	N
N	D	P	I	U	A	H	O	F	E	H	N	E	D
P	J	E	P	S	J	A	C	R	I	A	B	R	E
R	O	P	P	T	A	P	H	A	P	P	E	P	T
O	Y	A	Y	R	Y	P	O	I	L	Y	N	O	N
O	F	A	C	A	E	Y	P	D	U	M	E	D	O
B	U	P	O	T	S	S	T	O	N	R	R	I	T
O	L	I	N	E	T	A	S	K	I	A	G	R	I
R	N	U	T	D	A	N	D	E	B	N	E	M	R
E	N	T	E	X	C	I	T	E	D	G	T	O	E
D	H	U	N	G	R	Y	W	O	R	R	I	E	D
L	O	O	T	N	E	R	V	I	N	Y	C	D	D

Unit 11

Page 69

a. 7   b. 9   c. 8   d. 10   e. 4
f. 3   g. 6   h. 1   i. 2   j. 5

Challenge

1. T   2. T   3. F   4. b   5. F
6. F   7. c   8. F   9. T   10. a